EXECUTIVE ACHIEVEMENT

EXECUTIVE ACHIEVEMENT
MAKING IT
AT THE TOP

**ROBERT R. BLAKE AND
JANE S. MOUTON
SCIENTIFIC METHODS, INC.**

MCGRAW-HILL BOOK COMPANY
New York   St. Louis   San Francisco   Auckland
Bogotá   Hamburg   Johannesburg   London   Madrid
Mexico   Montreal   New Delhi   Panama   Paris
São Paulo   Singapore   Sydney   Tokyo   Toronto

Library of Congress Cataloging in Publication Data

Blake, Robert Rogers, date.
  Executive achievement.

  Includes bibliographies and index.
  1. Leadership.   I. Mouton, Jane Srygley.
II. Title.
HD57.7.B54   1985   658.4′092   85-16577
ISBN 0-07-005681-1

1234567890 DOC/DOC   898765

ISBN 0-07-005681-1

The editors for this book were William A. Sabin and Diane Krumrey, the designer was
Dennis Sharkey, and the production supervisor was Teresa F. Leaden. It was set in Basker-
ville by The Saybrook Press, Inc. Printed and bound by R. R. Donnelley & Sons Company.

CONTENTS

PREFACE

Industrial progress has begun to lag while technology is exploding in a thousand directions. Many critics and analysts trace the cause to leadership that has failed to keep pace. As a result, there have been few times in history when the topic of leadership has been of greater concern. What is leadership? How do you know when it's strong? What's the difference between strong and weak leadership? Can executives learn to be stronger leaders? Until these questions are answered, there is little possibility of selecting and promoting strong leaders, or of training people with responsibilities of leadership to increase their effectiveness.

The need for a book on leadership at this time is not demonstrated by any lack of publications on the subject; indeed, leadership has been discussed in two of the best-sellers of 1983. Most literature "talks" about it; some reports identify companies regarded highly for their leadership's quality. However, a large gap exists between writing about it and presenting an explicit model that demonstrates exactly the differences between effective and ineffective leadership.

This book presents a comprehensive theory of leadership that portrays ineffective and effective leadership at the highest levels of the organization. At this level leadership is most important to long-term corporate health because presidents, CEOs, and others at or near the top can exercise leadership with fewer constraints than managers lower in the organization. They can make things happen. When the phrase "the top leader" is used, it is the entire group of top people who are really being discussed.

Two chapters are interviews about effective leaders. The other six interviews concern executives who depart from effective leadership in varying degrees. These sketches allow the reader to see and feel each of the major styles rather than to read about them in an abstract way. The interviews are based on extensive examinations of great industrial entrepreneurs, from early in the twentieth century to the present: Ford, Sloan, Mellon, Carnegie, Procter, Watson, Shapiro of DuPont, Geneen of ITT, Ford II, Agee of Bendix, Welch of General Electric, Ackman of Superior Oil, and others. In addition, our personal acquaintanceships and interviews with many CEOs and presidents have permitted us to evaluate and corroborate the main themes. Over the years, we have known and worked with more than 200 members of the Young Presidents' Organization, which allowed us to observe and evaluate the key role that strong leadership contributes to a healthy corporate culture.

How is the exercise of leadership related to lowered profit, productivity, and quality in the performance of modern corporations? In searching for an answer, some leaders have concentrated their attention on the nuts-and-bolts side of running the business. How the nuts and bolts are dealt with is a function of leadership style and is the *content* side of leadership, which involves considerations such as strategic planning, financial analysis, knowledge of manufacturing, the ins and outs of marketing, and so on. Technical knowledge of how to run a business is necessary but insufficient in and of itself. When combined with strong leadership, any organization has a competitive edge.

The question is, How does any executive lead in working with and through others to solve the nuts-and-bolts problems? This is the *process* question. On the process side are such issues as how the leader interacts with subordinates and associates and how decisions are made, conflicts solved, creativity stimulated, and people motivated to commit their efforts to accomplishing organization purposes. The process side of leadership deals with human relationships: whether they are constructive and creative or whether they impede progress by making it difficult if not impossible for real content issues to be dealt with in a problem-solving way. The deep issue then is not that of achieving a balance between content and process but one of leaders becoming more skillful at the process of using business knowledge.

Some leaders say, "Look, I'm pretty successful. Why change a winning pattern?" Success is a relative matter. How much more successful might a person have been by shifting into a sounder style? That's the question.

Success needs to be evaluated more stringently than simply by measuring the bottom line. It ought to be considered in decade terms, not by the fiscal quarter. Factors that affect the real future ought to be geared into the assessment: creating talent for succession, providing capacity for innovation and regeneration, creating and maintaining high quality performance, developing a standard way for clearing out deadwood, and verifications of widespread involvement and commitment. That's how leadership affects corporate culture. Bottom line is one short-term measure, but it only adds up over years.

We offer a suggestion for how to get the most out of this book by the example of one of our most outstanding chief executives. Theodore Roosevelt tells how he read Sir John Morley's *Life of Gladstone*, a book about one of Britain's great statesmen. In a letter to Morley he said, "Of course, in reading the Gladstone, I was especially interested because of the ceaseless unconscious comparisons I was making with events in our own history, and with difficulties I myself every day encounter."[1]

This book provides the same opportunity to compare the style of these chief executives with your own approach to executive action at the top. Ask yourself, "Is this me? If so, why? Is it the best way to function? If not, how do I differ? Is that a superior approach to executive action?" Answers to these questions will provide numerous leads to self-improvement.

Its contribution to self-help and professional improvement has been reported by readers: "I never thought executives at high levels could appreciate and personally benefit from a self-help book." After reading through the various chapters, "I found a little bit of me in every chapter, but I stood out in one of them. That told me what I've got to do if I'm going to up my horsepower." "It made me realize I have not been asking enough in staff meetings I attend. I didn't have to be taught to ask questions; I knew that but hadn't been practicing it. This book pushed me in that direction." "I've not been really taking advantage of others who can contribute substantially to improving the decisions for which I am responsible. When I realized this, I began involving more of my executives in the deliberations that take place in our outfit." "I have strong convictions, but I have learned in the past to keep them to myself rather than making them known. I realize now that that's a mistake that I must rectify."

The book stimulates the reader to think about himself or herself as an executive leader: "my initiative," "my inquiry," "my advocacy," "my conflict solving," "my decision making," "my use of critique," and so on. Taking the book's message in this personal way results in substantial personal benefits. The theme is: self-help for the successful executive, or the better you are, the better you can get.

---

[1] Bishop, Joseph Bucklin, *Theodore Roosevelt and His Time*, vol. 1, Charles Scribner's Sons, New York, 1920, p. 269.

This book is organized into four major sections. Chapter 1 discusses the relationships between top leadership, corporate culture, and bottom-line results.

The question discussed in Chapter 2 is, How is effective leadership to be described? Chapter 3 presents an organized framework which enables the reader to compare one style of leadership with another.

Chapters 4 through 10 report studies of executives' leadership by concentrating on one leadership style in each chapter, showing how that leadership style permeated the organization culture and influenced the bottom line. Chapter 11 is a final study of executive leadership with particular emphasis on how the strategic model concept can have an impact on an organization.

The final section discusses organization change. Chapter 12 provides a stepwise model for the corporate pursuit of excellence, and Chapter 13 assesses the broader implications of increasing a corporation's capacity to be successful. The appendix is a technical treatment of the tactics of sound teamwork.

Robert R. Blake
Jane S. Mouton

EXECUTIVE
ACHIEVEMENT

1

CORPORATE CULTURE AND THE BOTTOM LINE

One key measure of making it at the top is the bottom line. The importance of the term *bottom line* is clear from its wide use in daily conversation. "What's the bottom line on that?" is frequently used, meaning "What's the payout?" Someone else says, "I'll give you the bottom line on that," meaning, "Let me tell you the results." Of course, everyone knows what bottom line is intended to mean when it comes to a financial statement.

By comparison, the words *corporate culture* have recently come into more widespread use but are far less understood. Yet there is a very direct relationship of cause and effect: corporate culture causes bottom line consequences.

The chief executive is a central influence on the corporate culture that emerges under his or her tenure and on the impact that this corporate culture has on the bottom line.

FACTORS INFLUENCING CORPORATE CULTURE

Some of the constantly operating factors of corporate culture are reasonably well identified, but none has achieved the attention it merits. For example, until the recent past, regulations have had a very controlling and constraining influence on businesses. Although many regulations were well intended, some have come to have such constricting effects that the natural evolution of business that might have emerged as a result of strong leadership often has been thwarted.

Another significant influence on corporate culture comes from technology and its ever-increasing significance on new products and processes, new ways of integrating information, and a host of developments almost too unbelievable to have been appreciated as little as fifteen or twenty years ago.

A third factor is the expectations of people. People in the sixties had quite different expectations, appreciations, and desires than either today or during the depression. Expectations, too, have an inherent influence on the shaping and reshaping of corporate culture.

A fourth factor is environmental conditions. Yesterday it was polluted water and air; today it is acid rain; tomorrow it may be hazards from heavy demands of industry and agriculture on water usage. Each environmental condition in turn becomes a source of influence on how business is, can, and should be conducted.

Still another influence on any corporation's culture comes from what competition is doing. Undoubtedly competitors play a critical role in how a company shifts its internal culture to meet the threat of destruction from without. Yesterday the focus was on domestic competition; today and tomorrow the threat from competition is and will be international in scope. There are dramatic examples in past years of how corporate cultures have been more or less totally reshaped by Japanese competition. Whole industries are being exported from the United States and the United Kingdom because of difficulties in retaining a competitive position. Intensification of competition can be expected to increase significantly over the next years, since it is widely acknowledged that the Japanese are aware of America's mounting industrial effort. For many companies the marketplace is now world-scale; it no longer is sufficient to think primarily of a domestic market or primarily of Europe. It is safe to assume that industrial corporations that practice world-scale marketing will have a great competitive advantage. A company that operates primarily within the United States can afford a changeover in models perhaps only every five years, but a manufacturer with a world market can afford to dominate the market by having a changeover far more often, such as on an annual basis. A company that modernizes its products every five years is at a significant competitive disadvantage over another one that is capable of doing so on a yearly basis.

Executive leadership is the most critical of all these factors of corporate culture. Executive leadership that is alive to possibilities can exploit technology, influence the commitments and involvements of its people, anticipate and therefore avoid becoming a victim of environmental conditions, and, in doing these things, maintain a competitive market advantage. Furthermore, if leadership does not recognize how these other factors affect the corporation, it is an evident truth that no other source of influence is available for getting on top and managing them well.

HOW LEADERS SHAPE CULTURE

It is one thing to say that leaders shape corporate culture but quite another to be specific about how this happens. Consider the following ways:

1. Leadership projects corporate vision. When organization members have a clear image of the corporate vision—what it is, where it wants to go, and how to get there—then the vision can be acted on in an intelligent manner by persons at all hierarchy levels.
2. Leadership provides a model that others emulate if they see it as sound, or renounce it if unsound.
3. Leadership establishes values that subordinates can be expected to embrace. If the values a leader lives by are perceived as shifty, tricky, and deceitful, there is likelihood that others will act according to these values as well. When a leader stands for integrity, is open and candid in expression, avoids running when disagreements and conflicts appear, and earns the respect of others by dedication to purpose, then conditions are created which shape organization culture in these directions.
4. Leadership sets or condones the reward system that compensates people. If these rewards are handed out in an arbitrary way or are based on favoritism, motivations unrelated to performance contributions come into play. If merit is the central criterion for determining appointments, succession, advancement, and so on, organization members realize that the main condition for success is corporate contribution.
5. Leadership sets policies by which an organization is expected to be conducted. Policies on employment, remuneration, real estate, retirement, research and development, centralization or decentrali-

zation—these and many more are basic to how well an organization is knitted together.

6. Leadership creates systems that influence how information flows, how work is undertaken, and other matters at the center of corporate culture.

7. One of the more often overlooked outcomes of a leader's influence is attitudes toward customers. This is reflected in a number of ways: quality, honoring delivery requirements, servicing after the sale, and so on. When a customer is seen as an inconvenience, inquiries are not answered, complaints are ignored, quality is disregarded, and customers turn to the competition.

8. Leadership demonstrated in decisions and attitudes toward excellence indicates how much mediocrity is to be tolerated. These subtle attitudes are red or green lights for "bad" or "good" actions.

9. Leadership can stimulate involvement and teamwork and promote sound use of human resources.

These and many other influences act on the organization from the executive suite. Of course, there are influences from lower components in the organization, and particularly so in more decentralized companies. However, since decentralization also starts at the top, it is correct to accord responsibility for these influences to top leadership.

It is not necessary to document the many influences that chief executives exert on the bottom line through corporate culture, though a few outstanding examples are well known. For example, Alfred P. Sloan became the head of General Motors when it was teetering on bankruptcy, enjoyed little more than 30 percent of market share, and had what was widely regarded as a dubious future. By comparison, Henry Ford, the founder, had brought the assembly line to Detroit, standardized parts, and conceived the manner in which unskilled people could be assigned to the assembly line. Ford was riding high and had 70 percent or so of the market. Yet in little more than ten years, the market share between General Motors and Ford was reversed. General Motors was on the way to becoming the world's industrial giant, and Ford was shutting assembly plants to determine how to meet the General Motors challenge.

What happened?

Close study of this turnaround leads to the conclusion that Henry Ford was a paternalist who failed to develop human resources. Sloan was probably this century's Number 1 industrial genius in shaping General Motors' corporate culture and developing an outstanding succession of persons capable of leading the corporation. Was any other factor as critical as executive leadership in making the difference?

In a similar manner the founders of Procter & Gamble brought ethical and moral persuasion into the value system of the company. Leadership gave Procter & Gamble a marketing edge in an area not then known for high technology and has been able to maintain that edge over many years. If the critical factor was not high technology, why was Procter & Gamble able to progress while others sank into oblivion?

A recent dramatic example is that of Sir Michael Edwardes. He successfully reversed a longtime downward trend of British Leyland, shifting it from the losing column to the prospects of its becoming a winner. Tom Watson, Sr., was the IBM leader in using the Hollerith card to record and code information and analyze data. With this core area of expertise, IBM technology has turned over repeatedly, but all the while the company has been able to maintain its dominating position in the data processing and interrelated fields. Is this leadership or luck? One would have to be arbitrary to ascribe this feat to the latter when the former seems so clearly responsible.

Leadership can also have a negative impact on corporate culture. We know that Bill Agee led Bendix to become embroiled in a bitter, ugly battle that forced Martin Marietta into a militant posture to protect itself from being taken over. The battle brought in United Technologies, and finally Bendix was gobbled up by Allied. Was this the product of executive leadership? or if not, what?

A recent example, now unfolding, is at ITT. Under Geneen's leadership, grueling headquarters sessions were conducted that called for the very best of inquiry and thoroughness from subordinates to avoid the terrible price paid for sloppiness. Geneen stepped down, and in a brief period ITT severely cut its dividend. Is that the price paid for dominating leadership? What other explanation could there be?

A final example is Continental Illinois, whose recent near-demise is perhaps the most obvious of the tragedies that have stalked the banking system.

These examples show there is every reason to concentrate on learning how a leader might become more effective with fuller understanding of what causes people to respond positively or negatively.

PATHS TO THE TOP

Since top leadership makes the critical difference in corporate culture, we might ask, "By the time they get to the top, are all executive leaders more or less alike in their exercise of leadership, or are there significant differences between one executive and another?" The argument that they become similar rests on the notion that a corporate culture depending on lower managers for job execution and higher managers for decisions results in a sorting-out process in which only the strong get to the top. This view has a certain solid basis. On the other hand, there are many routes to the top, and not all of them are based on a sound sorting-out process geared to achievement. A brief examination of some of the paths to the top will show the many-sided possibilities.

One is the path of technical competence. Land led Polaroid because he had the technological genius to create the instant camera. Thompson and Ramo were the scientists who rose to leadership at TRW. So technical competence comes into view as one, albeit not too common, factor in determining who enters the executive suite.

Other pathways to leadership are seniority, political skills, being a part of the old boy network, or being a protégé of a senior who in a parental way takes responsibility for advancing a "son" or "daughter" far beyond where everday comparisons of people might otherwise have taken them.

Some leaders are thrust into the top by circumstance: the plane crash that kills the chief executive, the unanticipated heart attack in an organization that does not have a succession program, and so on.

Another route to leadership is ownership. An industrial entrepreneur who establishes a company starts at the top. One may also become an owner by inheriting the organization as a property from one's forebears. Then there is always the case of marrying into the business.

Not yet mentioned is the critical role of positive leadership. Many observers feel that strong, positive leadership is perhaps the most critical and indispensable factor in corporate advancement regardless of how one gets to the top. Clearly, no amount of technical competence can bring about positive bottom-line results for a genius who makes enemies and depletes human resources. Advancement through seniority by no means ensures that those who have been in the organization the longest are the ones who can do best. Unanticipated circumstances, fate, and default are poor criteria, as is one's choice of a spouse. Industrial entrepreneurs often possess the indispensable ingenuity and energy for startup operations, but sometimes, as the company grows, they cannot "let go" enough to provide the necessary delegation.

A remaining leadership factor is merit. Merit truly relates to achieving bottom line outcomes with and through others and developing replenishable human talent over a long time horizon. The results obtained from such leadership concerns are genuine achievements and not products of the quick fix or of a management clearing house that brings dollars to the bottom line but depletes the organization of human resources necessary for long-term growth and development.

In the final analysis, leadership is everything. Because such importance is placed on leadership, it may be desirable to point out why it is such a critical variable in human performance. The reason is that the latest equipment, the best design, the best-constructed facilities, or even the most highly educated or most qualified personnel count for little or nothing if leadership falters. If leadership is ineffective, it is impossible to capitalize on the potentials that exist in a situation. It is in this sense that leadership is of central significance to organization effectiveness.

2

FACETS OF
LEADERSHIP
EFFECTIVENESS

Whenever two or more people are engaged in an activity, leadership involves determining a course of action while achieving coordination. The importance of leadership in our daily lives is difficult to overestimate. Its influence ranges through our vocabulary in such words as *king, tribal chief, president, boss, high priest, ayatollah, parent, general,* and *teacher*.

A recent conversation demonstrates the difficulty in trying to define what is meant by leadership.

> "What is the mission of your institution?" was the query put to an instructor at a military academy.
> "In the final analysis," he responded, "to train young people to lead."
> "But what does it mean to teach people to lead?"
> "It means leaders lead through the exercise of command," he observed.

"Can you explain that?"
"That's all there is to it. You can't take it any further. Leaders exercise command by leading."

This circular conversation portrays the conviction that leadership is a mystical, indescribable thing. We know better. Our goal here is to understand leadership by means of operational statements of concepts that represent leadership's more important aspects. These concepts can then be applied in order to understand what happens in actual relationships among people engaged in a shared activity. In the process of doing so, we wish to describe how to interpret these concepts and their implementation with regard to their impact on the bottom line.

Whether in business, industry, government, or academia, leaders achieve results with and through others. Whether called management, supervision, or administration, the underlying processes establish direction and the coordination in accomplishing results. In everyday settings the exercise of leadership may generate a range of emotional responses: enthusiasm, apathy, anger, commitment, complacency, indifference, or involvement. These varied emotions merely tell us that leadership is demonstrated in many different ways.

What an executive adds to his or her technical competence by way of leadership is critical to personal effectiveness. Strong, effective leadership arouses a high degree of involvement and shared commitment among those who work with and through one another. Under these conditions active participation in solving real issues assumes a key place in management activities because members have a clear sense of purpose. They give one another mutual support, which is indispensable to sound teamwork. They know what they're doing, and why, and are committed to its importance. The gains for profitable productivity are met, human benefits from meaningful involvement and commitment are available, and individual opportunities for advancement are increased. The process of exercising leadership creates a model for developing even better leadership in the future.

The exercise of effective leadership is a poorly understood process; however, it can be described by identifying six elements, or aspects of leadership. The element that stands out at any particular point depends on the problem being dealt with and the way in which the observer is looking at it. It is useful to think of facets of a diamond as a metaphor for leadership elements. When looked at from a certain angle, one element, or facet, stands out. When viewed from another angle, a different facet comes into sight. From a third, a still different leadership element may come into focus.

The first three elements, *initiative, inquiry,* and *advocacy,* reveal how a leader shapes his or her influences on outer events. The other three, *conflict solving, decision making,* and *critique,* are concerned with how the leader utilizes the resources of others with and through whom results are accomplished.

INITIATIVE

A leader exercises initiative whenever he or she concentrates effort on a specific activity—to start something, to stop something, or to shift the direction or character of a current activity. A description of initiative when it is exercised effectively is: "I exert vigorous effort and others join in enthusiastically." There are two words in this description that might be emphasized. One is *vigorous,* meaning strong, determined. The other is *enthusiastically.* Enthusiastic reactions indicate that others are caught up in the spirit of an activity; they throw themselves into it wholeheartedly to make a positive go of things.

When leadership is exercised in a vigorous way and others pick up the spirit of it and join in, much can be accomplished. The two parts of the preceding sentence cannot be separated without losing the meaning of effective initiative. If a leader exerts vigorous effort but others resist it or ignore it, then the obvious conclusion is that the initiative is ineffective.

INQUIRY

The leader needs to have a full and comprehensive grasp of the situations for which he or she is responsible. This involves the element of inquiry: thorough learning about the background and current status of problems, procedures, projects, and so on, and about the facts regarding the people involved in them, Without sound knowledge of situations in all these relevant aspects, it is clear that the exercise of leadership will be less effective than it might have been.

What is sound inquiry? An illustrative statement is: "I search for and validate information. I invite and listen for opinions, attitudes, and ideas different from my own. I continually reevaluate my own and others' facts, beliefs, and positions for soundness."

Inquiry can come from written or visual sources; from consulting books, texts, magazines, TV, or instructions; or from specific areas of corporate inquiry such as reports, special studies, financial statements, and so on. Also, conversations with others who are knowledgeable about the situation or who have some basis for evaluating it can contribute to the leader's understanding. Leaders probe associates for their information, opinions, and convictions regarding events and activities, solutions to problems, and opportunities for change. Thus, sound inquiry can provide the understanding essential to getting the best possible results.

ADVOCACY

Several people who are together in a working relationship are likely to have different points of view on how to approach or deal with various issues. *Advocacy* conveys the idea that the leader expresses his or her convictions and stimulates others to do likewise. All the members of the group let each other know where they stand, what they think, and how they feel about issues facing them.

Advocacy is important because it reflects one's view of things, one's vision of the future, one's thinking and judgment regarding issues and problems. It reveals the strength of convictions one places in conclusions reached. This aspect is of particular significance whenever an issue and its solution contain an element of risk. Advocacy can significantly reduce risk by testing possible solutions against the reasoning of several.

The statement that typifies effective advocacy is: "I feel it is important to express my concerns and convictions. I respond to ideas sounder than my own by changing my mind."

Advocacy is by no means always present to the degree that is desirable or necessary. For example, a person may have convictions but not express them or may be so bullheaded as to take positions with insufficient inquiry behind them so that the reaction produced is "he doesn't know what he's talking about."

CONFLICT SOLVING

Whenever an issue is complex and there is no self-evident solution, various participants are likely to have different perspectives on what to do. Such conditions often lead to conflict. The descriptive statement for effective conflict solving is: "When conflict arises, I seek out reasons for it in order to resolve underlying causes."

This approach permits conflict solving by getting to the roots of disagreement or controversy and reaching a solution based on understanding and agreement. The advantages are numerous, and yet it is noteworthy that this approach to conflict solving is rare. The main advantage comes from eliminating the source of tensions. In the absence of tensions, people can continue to deal with one another in an open way without withholding, ridiculing, manipulating, or being defensive.

DECISION MAKING

The acts most commonly associated with leadership involve making decisions. Decision making, however, can be no stronger than the initiative behind it, the inquiry on which it is based, the advocated positions which have been deliberated, and the resolution of disagreements and controversies through insight.

A descriptive statement of effective decision making is: "I place high value on arriving at sound decisions. I seek understanding and agreement." This statement characterizes strong leadership. It indicates that the leader places value on arriving at decisions, but not necessarily on making them alone. The leader may make decisions alone or, on the other hand, through thorough group deliberation so that everyone knows when the decision is made and yet no one can pinpoint any individual as having made it. The decision is more likely to be valid because it brings forth the best thinking possible. Widely deliberated issues, allowing the resolution of reservations and doubts, are likely to arouse widespread commitment to their implementation.

CRITIQUE

Critique means learning about how things have been done and how they or similar activities might be undertaken in a sounder manner in the future. When past experience proves sound, it becomes possible to get quicker results, to improve quality, to innovate—to do whatever is basic to success better than it has been done previously. The descriptive statement is: "I encourage two-way examination of how we do things in order to strengthen operations."

Critique frequently is confused with criticism, but the two are not the same. Criticism implies evaluation and judgments of good or bad, relative to personal worth. Critique involves learning from experience what is sound and what is unsound. Criticism is person-centered, while critique is work-centered. In the latter case people are studying how to increase their effectiveness.

SUMMARY

These six elements represent the key facets of effective leadership. Now it is possible to examine what is implied by the use of the word *effective* in the context of effective leadership. There are several aspects.

Effective leadership means finding sound solutions to problems and engaging in innovative activities that are productive, creative, and pertinent to the organization purpose. It conveys the notion that such leadership is being exercised in ways that develop people and that minimize the expense of doing business.

For leadership to be truly effective, it has to solve current problems without creating additional ones. Yet we know that many times leaders engage in solving problems in such a way as to produce new and even more serious problems in the future. In other words, a longer time perspective is essential for assessing whether effective leadership is being exercised. As important as time perspective is, another essential feature of effective leadership is that it replenishes and replaces itself. People who observe effective leadership in action learn from this experience how to exercise it themselves.

The Grid in Chapter 3 provides a framework for gauging top leadership effectiveness and ineffectiveness. We outline seven distinctive patterns of leadership and trace the consequences of each when exercised over sufficient time to affect corporate culture and the bottom line.

THE GRID®

Sound leadership produces organizational success. Unsound leadership results in failure. Training in financial analysis, by itself, may be desirable, but when this knowledge is employed by a leader using faulty leadership, financial analysis leads nowhere. The same goes for any other subject matter that enters into business decisions, whether it is law, engineering, a scientific discipline, manufacturing know-how, or high technology. While knowledge of these disciplines may be indispensable to good decision making, these competencies by no means assure solid decisions.

The Leadership Grid, as shown in the accompanying figure, is a systematic way of analyzing underlying patterns that exist in different people as they exercise initiative, inquiry, advocacy, and so on. In other words, the Grid gives a comprehensive approach to seeing different manifestations of leadership in a coherent way. A comprehensive review of the research evidence underlying the Grid is available elsewhere.[1,2]

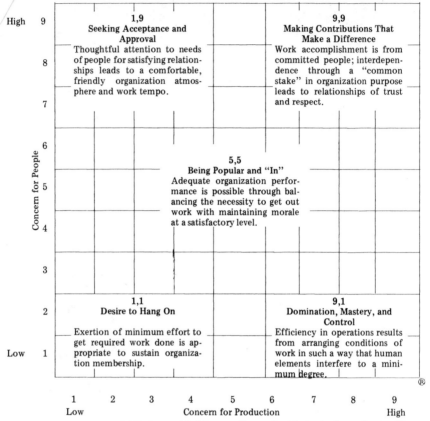

<table>
</table>

High 9	**1,9** **Seeking Acceptance and** **Approval** Thoughtful attention to needs of people for satisfying relation- ships leads to a comfortable, friendly organization atmos- phere and work tempo.	**9,9** **Making Contributions That** **Make a Difference** Work accomplishment is from committed people; interdepen- dence through a "common stake" in organization purpose leads to relationships of trust and respect.

5,5
Being Popular and "In"
Adequate organization performance is possible through bal-
ancing the necessity to get out
work with maintaining morale
at a satisfactory level.

1,1
Desire to Hang On

Exertion of minimum effort to
get required work done is appropriate to sustain organization membership.

9,1
Domination, Mastery, and
Control
Efficiency in operations results
from arranging conditions of
work in such a way that human
elements interfere to a minimum degree.

Concern for People — High 9, 8, 7, 6, 5, 4, 3, 2, Low 1

1   2   3   4   5   6   7   8   9
Low   Concern for Production   High

The Leadership Grid® (*R. Blake and J. Mouton, Scientific Methods, Inc., Austin, Texas,*
1985. Reproduced by permission.)

The Grid is a two-dimensional framework. *Concern for production,*
that is, getting results, is one dimension. The second is *concern for*
people—superiors, colleagues, and subordinates with and through whom
one achieves results. *Concern* is not a mechanical term which indicates
literal production or actual conduct toward people. Rather, it indicates
the character or strength of assumptions behind any given leadership
approach.

Concern for Production

A key executive may demonstrate concern for production (or for results,
bottom line, performance, profits, or mission) by finding new directions
for the growth through acquisitions or by launching or expanding innovative research and development. Concern for production covers both

quantity and quality. It may be revealed in the scope and validity of decisions, the number of creative ideas that product development converts into salable items, the accounts processed in a collection period, or the quality and thoroughness of services provided.

Where work is physical, concern for production may take the form of efficiency measurements, number of units produced, time required to complete a certain production run, volume of sales, or attainment of a specified quality level. In a government agency, productivity measures may be mail delivery time, number of forms correctly processed, or number of union-management conflicts brought to successful resolution through mediators. Production, in other words, is whatever an organization employs people to accomplish.

Concern for People

Since executives get results with and through others, the assumptions they make about people are important in determining effectiveness. People are people regardless of the context in which the work takes place—industry, government, education, or medical institutions.

Concern for people is revealed in many different ways. Some leaders show their concerns in efforts to ensure that subordinates like them. Others are concerned that subordinates get their jobs done. Efforts at getting results, whether based on trust and respect, obedience, sympathy, or understanding and support, are manifestations of concern for people. Policies regarding working conditions, salary structure, fringe benefits, job security, and so on also demonstrate a leader's concerns, or lack of them. The degree of concern includes both character and intensity. Depending on the character of concern, subordinates may respond with enthusiasm or resentment, involvement or apathy, innovative or dull thinking, commitment or indifference, and eagerness or resistance to change.

How These Concerns Relate to One Another

The Grid measures these concerns on a nine-point scale. 1 represents low concern, 5 represents an average amount of concern, and 9 is high concern. The other numbers, 2 through 4 and 6 through 8, denote intermediate degrees. However, these points signify steps between low and high just as the gauge in an automobile indicates the relative amount of fuel from empty to full, rather than specific quantities.

The manner in which a leader addresses these two concerns, for production and for people, defines the quality of how his or her authority is used. For example, when high concern for people is coupled with a low concern for production, the leader wants people to be contented. This is far different from a high concern for people coupled with a high concern for production. Here the leader wants people to be involved in the work and to strive enthusiastically to contribute.

While there are numerous ways of uniting these two concerns, eight styles are especially important for understanding leadership. Each of these styles rests on a different set of assumptions about how power and authority are used to link people into production. The actual processes are revealed in initiative, inquiry, advocacy, conflict solving, decision making, and critique. Before examining these styles, however, let us define *motivation* and *option*.

Motivations include what a person strives to reach as well as what a person seeks to avoid. Therefore we can show motivation measured on a scale having end points of plus (+) and minus (−) with gradations of intensity between them. The motivational end points differ for each of the Grid styles of leadership.

In working with and through other people, a leader needs to be aware of available options in ways to lead. An option is a way of thinking about or analyzing a problem, an orientation that is changeable. To increase managerial competence, the leader needs to know these various orientations and to select from among them the best way to exercise leadership. From the range of orientations, eight display significant differences in characteristic actions and outcomes. They are benchmark styles.

Five "Pure" Styles

9,1   In the lower right-hand corner a maximum concern for production (9) is combined with a minimum concern for people (1). Dictating to subordinates what they should do and how they should do it, the leader concentrates on maximizing production.

1,9   In the top left is 1,9 leadership style. The leader shows a minimum concern for production (1) but a maximum concern for people (9). Even at the expense of achieving results, fostering good feelings gets primary attention.

1,1   In the lower left, position 1,1 represents minimum concern for both production and people. The leader with a 1,1 orientation puts forth only the least effort required to remain within the organization.

5,5   The center depicts the 5,5 orientation. This is the middle-of-the-road style or the go-along-to-get-along attitude that results in conformity to the status quo.

9,9   The upper right represents the 9,9 style, which integrates production and people concerns at a high level. This is the team approach. It is goal-centered and seeks results through the participation, involvement, and commitment of all those who can contribute.

These five patterns encompass the more important Grid styles found among executives. Intermediate degrees, such as 9,5; 5,9; 8,3; or 4,4 represent style mixtures. Most of the benefits to be gained from discussing styles of intermediate Grid locations do not seem worth the complexities involved in specifying their characteristics.

Other Grid Styles

Paternalism, opportunism, and "facadism" are different combinations of the underlying assumptions in two or more basic Grid styles.

Paternalism. An arc between the 9,1 and 1,9 corners connects high concern for production with high concern for people in an additive way. Compliance to the leader's directions by subordinates receives the boss's approval, and noncompliance brings forth criticism and reprimand.

Opportunism. This style occurs when three or more Grid styles are used interchangeably, depending on the person with whom the leader is dealing. A 1,9 approach is used in ingratiating oneself with important people; 5,5 ways of doing favors to obligate people are used with colleagues or equals; and 9,1 domination and mastery serve to control subordinates.

Facadism. A facade is a form of deception used to hide one's true intentions in order to achieve by indirect means something one believes unattainable if one's true Grid style were known. The "front" is usually a 9,9 orientation to hide a 9,1, paternalist, or opportunist style.

It is important to understand that there is no close relationship between IQ and Grid style. Intelligent as well as less intelligent people utilize all Grid styles. To say it another way, a 1,9-oriented executive may be no less intelligent than a 9,1- or a 9,9-oriented manager. IQ is important to effectiveness, but it contributes little to improve an ineffective Grid style. Thus, the Grid is a set of theories about how people use whatever intelligence and skills they have in working with and through others.

Dominant and Backup Assumptions

Any Grid style is a set of assumptions that tell the executive what to do. They may lead to sound or unsound behavior, but the assumptions determine behavior. If behavior were unrelated to assumptions, it would be random and purposeless and not make any sense or be predictable. Leaders seldom verbalize their assumptions, but they do act on them. Only by learning what his or her assumptions are does it become possible for a leader to recognize other assumptions that might strengthen leadership behavior.

Granted that an executive's Grid style may be consistent over a range of situations, it is also true that managers move from one Grid style to another. Sometimes executives shift and adapt Grid styles according to how they feel on a given morning. Sometimes an executive may appear to exercise initiative in a 5,5 manner and yet meet situations of conflict with more of a 1,9 approach.

How can the concept of a dominant set of assumptions be reconciled with difference, shift, and change? Most executives have not only a dominant Grid style but also a backup style, sometimes even a third and fourth. An executive's backup style becomes apparent when it is difficult or impossible to apply the dominant Grid style because it doesn't work. A backup style is the style a leader reverts to, particularly when under pressure, tension, or in situations of conflict that cannot be solved in more characteristic ways.

Connections between dominant and backup styles are visible, for example, in how executives deal with recalcitrant subordinates. First they may try logic and reason in a 9,9 way. If the tactic doesn't work, they adopt a get-tough approach, possibly with a touch of ridicule. Both are 9,1 ways of attempting to get obedience. Since they have created resentment and rejection, they switch to friendliness and encouragement with the hope that this 1,9 attitude will bring a subordinate around. Still unable to elicit cooperation, the executive may either return to a 9,1 strategy of threats and punishments or may withdraw in a 1,1 way and say, "Forget it. It's not worth worrying about."

It is important to remember that the style or styles employed by people as they work can be complex. The dominant or most characteristic style is the one most central to understanding how a person manages. The dominant style may not always be the one first evident in a given situation. For example, a manager might begin a meeting with subordinates in a friendly and casual way but quickly utilize a 9,1 approach when they get down to business. Even though the friendly, casual beginning might be 1,9 in character, the 9,1 approach is the dominant one. The backup is the one used next most often as the basis for actions. To understand dominant and backup approaches it is necessary to observe behavior over time and over a range of situations. Some managers shift frequently and others less often.

Many times a leader is confronted with dilemmas with which there seems no way of coping. In these situations, little can be done other than to try one thing and then another, and this may lead to a shift from a dominant to a backup strategy.

Any Grid style can back up any other. For example, a 1,9-oriented leader prefers to yield but may become stubborn and demanding (9,1) when the pressure becomes too great. A leader who seeks control and mastery in a 9,1 way and meets continued resistance from subordinates may shift to a 9,9 teamwork basis. A dominant to backup shift also may occur when an executive works with subordinates in a 9,9 manner in everyday situations but then switches when crises arise. A 9,1 backup appears when the executive takes over an operation without utilizing the resources of those who may be best able to contribute to a solution. The great array of dominant-backup combinations is what makes each person unique.

SELF-DECEPTION

It might seem that the most straightforward way to find out how leaders lead is to ask them. Who knows better what they are trying to do and why?

Contradictory to common sense though it is, the straightforward way turns out to be not the best but close to the worst way of getting the right answer. What is the best source? If not the leader, then who is? Why are leaders a poor source of insight into their own leadership?

There are several reasons. One is that hierarchy gets in the way of self-assessment, and the higher a person's position the more it gets in the way. The question is, how? The observation that "the higher the rank of the boss, the funnier the jokes" or "the higher the rank of the boss, the more profound the pronouncements" tells the story. It's the emperor's clothes all over again.

As bosses rise in rank, they come to be held in awe. What foreman is going to tell the president that the jokes are flat or pronouncements off target? Negative feedback is shut off, not by the leader's intention but by those lower in rank withholding it. This means what the boss is likely to be getting is feedback contradictory to objective facts. If the laughter gets louder, the boss is being told, in effect, "Your humor is really appreciated."

Another source of this blind spot is that leaders pay attention to what they think are their good intentions, though these often are not their real intentions. People want to think they are well-intentioned even though bad or negative intentions may hold sway. For example, a leader may deny a subordinate a promotion. The rationalization is that "he has simply not delivered what I expected of him," or "she still has more to learn in this position," when the underlying intention may be to let the subordinate know in no uncertain terms that the boss finds him or her personally repugnant. The boss may say, "I'm doing it for your own good; you need more time to prove yourself," rather than trying to become aware of what's operating beneath the surface.

The depth of the problem of self-deception has been brought to the fore in a recent *Fortune* study.[3] Ten top leaders described themselves in personal interviews, and then subordinates described the same leaders. One example will illustrate the problem.

Here's how Martin Davis, chief executive of Gulf & Western, sees himself:

> "I am tough. . . . I'm a team player. I don't want people weaker than I am."

Others say about him:

> "Probably one of the most demanding people in the world. Yells, curses when he chews people out. . . . Employees all scared to death of him."

This example, which is more typical than not, shows significant differences between how this chief executive sees himself and how he is viewed by associates.

Why do executives, who pride themselves on calling it as it is, kid themselves? There are several reasons. One is that we take for granted the things we do day in, day out. They become second nature. We know ourselves so well superficially that at a deeper level we don't know ourselves at all. Second, we do many things to provide ourselves false explanations for our actions in order to feel pleased with ourselves. Leaders who chew out subordinates never learn what others think about them. Leaders who are easily offended or hurt give off signals that say, "Don't tell me anything unless you tell me something nice about me." Leaders who have gone to sleep on the job aren't listening and therefore don't hear what they may need to know. Leaders who buy the status quo lock, stock, and barrel take offense from anyone who suggests change. Paternalists draw around them people with worshipful attitudes that blind leaders to flaws they might have. Opportunists are masters at telling others what they want to hear, not what they need to know. All these behaviors can work hand-in-glove with one another and produce massive self-deception, with leaders in the center of something they think they understand but often do not.

One solution to self-deception is for leaders to rely on second persons to help them see themselves. This solution can provide invaluable learning because it helps leaders see the consequences of their leadership.

Sketches of leaders, whose careers as chief executives are to be reviewed on a chapter-by-chapter basis, make effective or ineffective leadership apparent. These sketches allow the reader an inside view in order to promote some understanding of what motivated the exercise of leadership as it was employed, to show how the executive thought about achieving production with and through others, and to clarify in specific and concrete terms why some failed while others succeeded.

This study presents a comprehensive theory. The objective is to gain an intimate view of a number of chief executives and the six key leadership facets of their performance. At the end of each of these chapters, descriptive summaries of the six elements illustrate the specific Grid style revealed in the leader's behavior.

The objective is to provide the executive a means for seeing what really is involved, the conceptual basis for separating strong from weak leaders, and suggestions for strengthening leadership throughout an entire organization.

The primary source material is a set of interviews with persons who have had years of experience working with the executives being described. The interviewer in Chapters 4–11 is Walt Burton.

The main questions to ask in reading each chapter are:

1. What are the individual and organizational conditions which create, reinforce, and permit a given leadership style to continue?
2. What are the organizational consequences of such behavior by the chief executive?
3. How can an executive who leads in this manner change in order to become more effective?

Answering these questions provides the keys to strengthening performance at all levels and to gaining better organization results.

REFERENCES

1. Robert R. Blake and Jane S. Mouton. *The Managerial Grid III: The Key to Leadership Excellence*, Gulf Publishing Company, Houston, 1985.
2. Robert R. Blake and Jane S. Mouton. *Corporate Excellence through Grid Organization Development*, Gulf Publishing Company, Houston, 1968. Revised 1986 edition in press.
3. Steven Flax. "The Toughest Bosses in America," *Fortune*, vol. 110, no. 3, August 1984, pp. 18–23.

4

SOLVING TOMORROW'S PROBLEMS TODAY

"Thanks, Andy, for making this time available to discuss George Thomas," said Walt Burton. "I think a good place to start would be to tell me about your association with him."

"We've both been in this company for 20 years," Andy Ling began. "Of that time we've been close friends for about seven. I am one of three vice presidents reporting to him. The other two are Anne Ryan and Frank Johnson. Frank has been a source of many stormy conflicts as head of new product development. He has recently been terminated, as well as Ben Davis, the president of one of our subsidiaries in Europe. That episode may be of interest to you because it had wide media coverage."

"I suggest we start with how you view Thomas as chief executive. What has he tried to achieve?"

"Well," said Andy, "I'll put it in personal terms first and then discuss it from the standpoint of corporate action.

"On the positive side I have seen him striving to leave the situation in a significantly better condition than when he started. Many of his actions have brought attention to him, but notoriety was not his motivation. Some even aroused quite a bit of controversy and polarization within the company. When it came down to the bottom line, he did things because they were right. It sounds contradictory to say so, but he is a man without an ego; he is dedicated to doing what needs to be done."

"Are you saying that you haven't seen him do things just to make himself look good or to prove he was right for the sake of proving it?"

"Exactly," replied Andy. "He identifies with the corporation as a living, vital institution. I've heard him say, 'The only security for employees and stockholders is in our being strong, sound, and competitive and making our corporation as excellent as we can.' In this sense, he looks from a long-range perspective regarding the health of the corporation. He sets his priorities on the basis of what will give us the maximum strength for facing the future."

"That's an interesting statement of values. While media accounts place a different emphasis upon some of his actions, your remarks certainly provide a strong basis for seeing Mr. Thomas in the larger context."

"Before we get into further explanation of how he managed the corporation," said Andy, "let me give you what I think might be the key to the man's leadership. Upon taking over his job, he said in a conversation with Frank, Anne, and me, 'Our job is, on the one hand, to identify our corporate strengths and increase them and, on the other, to find every drag factor that reduces corporate vitality and eliminate it. This means I will be facing, and asking you to face, many issues that will require our sustained effort to resolve. I'd like to ask you to think about our jobs and we'll have another session next week. I don't have the right to insist or to demand you take this job on with me, but I do have the right to ask you to join with me if you are capable of giving it enthusiastic commitment.' "

"Can you tell me what he has sought to avoid from a managerial point of view?" asked Walt.

"That's a little harder. Basically, I would say that he has tried to avoid doing things that would be for merely his personal interests and ambitions.

"There's a subtle angle," continued Andy. "I have seen a number of senior people lose perspective on themselves in a way that causes them trouble. They come to accept their treatment as office holders as their just deserts for being important people. George never makes that blunder.

"Let me give you an illustration," continued Andy. "One of the questions that had been debated was concerned with corporate aircraft. They certainly are a status item, and under certain conditions can be a cost-reducer, particularly if there are large numbers of personnel moving between distant locations difficult to reach by commercial airlines. But then, of course, it becomes something of a scheduled corporate airline and that's not what I'm talking about. The question was: should we have corporate aircraft assigned and restricted to the use of senior executive officers and board members, plus significant visitors and important clients? It was a legitimate question not only because corporate officers need the convenience but also because it is possible for several officers to conserve time by working on a corporate jet. So the resolution of the matter came about through a study that examined convenience in the context of cost-effectiveness. The conclusion was that we couldn't possibly match the convenience or cost-effectiveness provided by commercial airlines. The pomp and ceremony of a personal jet did build status with chief executive officers from other companies, but because it contributed little to operational effectiveness he termed it selfish. It's a gray area item, of course, because there are some perks that are more black and white than that. Our retreat in Idaho and a permanently rented suite of rooms at the Waldorf are examples of perks that have no clear relevance to profitability."

"His motivation is to contribute rather than look out for himself. How do you relate these motivations to corporate performance?" asked Walt.

"It's not all that difficult," said Andy. "Contribution means taking the larger view and seeing what needs to be done from the standpoint of the health of the corporation. I think he's always been oriented this way. I recall arguments when we were both process engineers just after finishing chemical engineering degrees.

"He was a refinery engineer assigned to a design project for a small new plant to be built within the refinery complex. We wanted this plant for our own refinery. We also knew a sister refinery wanted it and had certain advantages of feed stock and transportation we were in no position to match. However, we did have a better reputation for construction and maintenance. In fact, I think we were probably viewed at the time, and correctly so, as the finishing school of the system in the sense that many managers and executives, including George and me, emerged from our refinery and advanced into top positions in the company. So, from one standpoint we couldn't match certain advantages the other refinery had, and the advantages we had were distinctly in the human and management areas.

"He got our design group and the refinery manager involved in discussion: whether we should drive to get the project because we'd be better off with it or whether we were free to take an objective view in the light of corporate interests. It was a tough discussion. For at least a period of time he was regarded as a traitor arguing on behalf of the enemy. Our design group was a group of dedicated people, and while we felt competitive, we finally found it possible to put dedication above winning."

"So what happened?"

"When our design group met at headquarters with the design group from the other refinery, you could feel tension. We wanted it, but it was obvious that they wanted it, too.

"We went with the instruction to argue our case on its merits alone. We kept slipping into negative comments and invidious comparisons, but eventually we acknowledged the net merit of the plant's being built in the other refinery. The other design group didn't expect this admission, of course, and in effect our own design group agreed, after the fact, that we felt better for having done the right thing rather than having simply fought a battle. It was George who led us to see the corporate rather than refinery interests. That's contribution and avoidance of selfishness.

"Back at our refinery, people were disappointed, but the disappointment soon passed. Another project came under review for construction and it was obvious that for this one we did have the cost advantage viewed in corporate terms. We got it and built it, and that unit continues to operate even today."

"You said you have seen George operating in this way on a consistent basis throughout his career?"

"Yes," said Andy. "As you know, his career has been a striking one, and there have been many hard-fought battles in this company. George doesn't hesitate to take on a problem just because it's big or because it's risky, with an unforeseeable outcome. I think these battles have been the critical difference between our success in financial and other measures and that of our competitors, who have not done as well. The comparison is pretty straightforward."

"In one respect, you might conclude that corporate leadership is a matter of exercising initiative. How would you describe him in that context?"

"George's initiative can be viewed in two ways, I suppose. From one standpoint it's an individual matter, and he certainly has launched many activities in this company, which may be one key to the liveliness of the organization now. But it's not the sole key because when you look from another angle, individual initiative has come to be a widespread phenomenon in our organization. He has led the exercise of initiative, but certainly others also have taken the lead and have become highly involved and responsible for exercising strong effort. I suspect others' taking initiative comes from the fact that he has led the way. Somehow or other, we all have successfully achieved a high level of corporate commitment.

"Over this decade we have shifted our promotion system away from an excessive reliance on a seniority, 'old boy' network. We were okay, but George felt this area needed attention to develop strength to meet future requirements. We now have a talent bank of human resource competencies available throughout the corporation.

"The initial formulation met with reservations and doubts, particularly from the old guard. The reservations were not against merit as a principle. They came from people who had become conditioned to the organization culture: a lot of fair-haired types produced by a self-serving mentoring system, some 'old boys' interested in mutual back-scratching, and some with the motto 'who you know, not what you know.' Before anything much could be done to shift, we had to prove to ourselves that we were often merely giving lip service to merit. We worked it through at the top level first, including the various vice presidential-level people and, of course, the vice president of human resources.

"The point is that George might have taken the route of outlining a merit-based performance program and delegating it to Stan, the VP of human resources. Had he done so, I think we would have made very little progress. Stan had as much of the old boy network embedded in his own personal corporate history as others who also had come up through the system. It was only by getting all of us, particularly the line people, behind the idea that it was possible for Stan to take the lead in designing a merit-based performance appraisal approach and getting a training program organized that whittled down resistance at all levels before making any effort to give people greater skills than they previously had. Now we are operating under a first-rate merit program, including the talent bank I mentioned. Once a year it gets a major policy review and an operational checkup looking for weaknesses, breakdowns, and departures from it."

"I'd like to ask you to describe it," said Walt. "However, I can get that from others, so we ought to move on. The next area to explore is the gathering of information. Keeping informed can be very important in effective leadership. I see this as important, since decision making can only be as sound as the information on which it is based. How would you picture George's approach?"

"What has to be understood," responded Andy, "is George's attitude toward thoroughness. He conducts himself, and expects others to do so for that matter, according to a high standard of thoroughness. As the basis for decisions he wants to know why something is a problem, how it came about, as well as how to solve it. George says, 'Let's get it right the first time.' That's his thoroughness.

"George studies the company just like anything else. He's an avid reader of business magazines and trade journals and digests the contents of internal documents, memos, reports, and so on.

"I can't tell you how he does it, but he has the same attitude toward studying people. He keeps a sharp eye focused on what people propose and how the proposals actually turn out over a series of occasions. I know he monitors integrity, and it is one of his primary tests of character. This is important because he often asks other people in whom he has implicit trust to gather information for him as well as to represent him in complex negotiations and situations he is unable to attend to personally.

"This reminds me of one of the few times I really saw him lose his temper, which is rare in the first place. His composure cracked because the situation violated his deepest sense of values.

"He found out the vice president of strategic planning had taken credit for a proposal that benefited the company quite handsomely. It had originally been proposed by a young manager down the line. When George got wind of it, he went directly to the VP and let him have it. He later admitted he flew off the handle but, as I said, he can't tolerate lack of integrity in himself or others. Subsequently he and the VP talked it through."

"You mentioned earlier about the exchange of information among executive committee members," said Walt.

"I said he wants key people to be informed as generalists over and above their specialties. He leads the way by inquiring into topics far removed from chemical engineering, manufacturing, or financial analysis. He's a great questioner, as a matter of fact, enjoying open-ended, freewheeling give-and-take as much as precise, detailed, or linear analysis.

"He also has respect for fresh information that is firsthand. He's constantly arranging trips and visits to various locations, and it's interesting to observe how he conducts himself on these occasions. He calls on the top man first, but then, if conferences have not been prearranged, he arranges them then and there to study special problems, issues, or circumstances. He expects these discussions to be as full and frank as those in headquarters. I think he is studying the top man he is visiting to assess the openness and candor that prevails between him and subordinates and among subordinates. He also sees these trips as important opportunities to communicate values he wishes more fully to be respected as aspects of corporate culture."

"Anything else about getting information?" asked Walt.

"It's true that everyone has to act and make decisions beyond the information given. George sees that as the nature of the management task. But many times a large gap prevails between available and used information. This is the gap that George tries to keep as closed as possible.

"Much of this is done by communication between those who share responsibilities. We are a very talking organization, exchanging information which is both of direct interest and of background pertinence. George wants the executives with whom he works to be as fully informed on everyone else's activities as possible, but I'll talk more about that if we get into how we make decisions around here."

"It's one thing for people to have a thorough basis of knowledge from sound inquiry, and another to use it wisely. What about advocacy, particularly when a point of view does not necessarily earn the endorsement of everyone?"

"One outstanding thing characterizes George's style of advocacy," said Andy. "It's candor. He tells the truth—tells it like it is. I want to say absolute candor, but I suspect that's more candor than anyone can expect. You get the notion, as far as work-related matters are concerned, that he is straightforward and frank and expects the same from those with whom he carries out discussions. If they have a different point of view from his, it's their obligation to make their viewpoint clear. The reason is that the soundness of his decision is limited by the extent to which others help him by expressing their reservations, doubts, and disagreements. Without that help, the rest of the system breaks down because it becomes political in character."

"Doesn't that produce hopeless controversy?" asked Walt.

"No, it doesn't, and there are several reasons for that. One is that we fully expect people to express not only their beliefs but also their reservations and doubts. Second, George does the same as he expects of others. It is not that he is a passive listener while others speak their minds. It's an open situation among us all. This stimulates the candor that is characteristic of this group. When we had worked through—as we had—this issue of serving the larger interest rather than dealing from the angle of personal gain, we realized that when someone differs with us it was less likely now to be based on a win-or-lose attitude or on chemistry. There is an important distinction between operationally sound advocacy and conflict resolution. That's another topic, although they're related, of course."

"Let's move on and talk about that. What's George's view and how does he deal with conflict?" asked Walt.

"First of all, I think his leadership ability reduces the amount of conflict he has to contend with. Nonetheless, we do have conflicts.

"The way he has gone about trying to resolve conflict is what you are interested in, so let me try to describe it. One thing we routinely do is to step away from the problem itself and try to identify the ideal solution as contrasted with practical ones. Sometimes we've relieved conflicts by finding out how to change actual circumstances to bring them into line with the best solution possible.

"Conflicts remain in spite of all that. I'll track a couple and give you my version of how he goes about relieving them.

"I mentioned he came into the presidential office and became chief operating officer at a young age. He advanced into the chairmanship and became chief executive officer at an age younger than is normative in industry, thirty-eight as a matter of fact. I mention this because of a situation it created for him.

"A certain inherent problem is likely to be created when you jump the shoulders of the other people. For example, Ben Davis, the president of the subsidiary operating in Europe, fifteen years his senior, reacted to George's elevation as a threat to his own future. Ben was a regional president, with the various national companies of Europe reporting to him in the London headquarters, but that shift in title had not as yet been made clear during the episode I'm talking about.

"Circumstances were such that he hadn't made the personal acquaintance of George for almost a year and a half after George took over. George felt there was something of a standoff, but this notion was more inferential than evidence-based. Finally George decided that he should become acquainted with Ben on a firsthand basis. He explored with immediate subordinates in New York the best time to have Ben come to the Avenue of the Americas.

"We felt that Ben had avoided or at least found excuses for not making a corporate visit for some time and that because of his outstanding operation in Europe, he might create quite a stir in New York. A stir was not intended; George simply wanted to get to know Ben. George decided that he would tour Europe along with Ben. Jointly they would visit and have informal reviews with the various national presidents as to how they viewed the political scene, national economic developments, and so on— the kind of thing you can sometimes get best on a firsthand basis. That sort of discussion loses a good deal when summarized and reported in charts, data, and statistics.

"George wrote, requesting that Ben set up arrangements for the visit, but Ben resisted. George couldn't accept his reasons, which were that Ben had already made a series of commitments for the designated period and it would be inconvenient for him to join George. George let this pass and searched for other dates. It seemed that no mutually convenient date could be found.

"At this point George felt that something more was involved than appeared on the surface. So he wrote, saying, 'I have made several proposals, and none has been acceptable. I find it important to make your acquaintance and to become more familiar with activities in Europe. Therefore, I will be in your headquarters on March 1, three months away, and I feel sure that you will be able to reschedule your activities to make this visit mutually gainful.'

"George did not hear either way. Ben didn't say he couldn't make it, nor did he say, 'Fine.'

"George was not about to probe further for an explanation, and so on March 1 he appeared in London and phoned. Ben was unavailable, but no explanation was offered. So he said to Ben's assistant, 'I'm in London. I want you to contact him. I expect to meet him today. When he arrives at headquarters, I wish that fact to be made known to me, and at that time I will take next steps.' The call came at 3:00 p.m. Ben was all sweetness and light—no apology, just very gracious.

"Now, what I've described was inappropriate behavior, but recall that Ben was George's senior by fifteen years and undoubtedly felt his career had been jeopardized by George's elevation. George felt that while Ben's behavior was unacceptable he ought to gain more background on it before taking any action. He already had reviewed this with the Board, which gave its support for his trying to get to the root cause of the behavior.

"The schedule of visits to the various companies was completed. Ben's and George's conversations were not very analytical or evaluative. George found it difficult to get Ben to open up to the implications of angles that were brought up during these discussions. The best he could get from Ben would be something like, 'Oh, I think it's all right,' or, 'Yes, I'll look into that.' He never got anything like, 'What do you think?' or 'How would you suggest that I might deal with this one?' In other words, Ben admitted no problems and asked no advice."

"In some respects that sounds like the ultimate in conflict," said Walt. "You can't get through to him because he resists, and he in turn makes no effort to open up. What was the outcome?"

"George summed up actions that he thought should be placed on his agenda—information he needed, things he wanted Ben to look into, and so on. He took the initiative to stop certain significant budget items from being further twisted into various unapproved uses. He also confronted Ben with his own tensions and opened the door for Ben to vent any feelings he had toward George, but to no avail."

"What did Ben say?"

"Ben said he understood what George wanted, and he did not voice disagreement. It was appropriate for George to take his acknowledgement of understanding as agreement with the requests.

"A very interesting thing happened three months later. George learned that Ben had continued unauthorized expenditures George had told him should be discontinued."

"How did George interpret that?"

"It wasn't a matter of interpretation any longer. It was the basis for a conclusion. The only conclusion that could be drawn was that George had used sound logic to draw the line, and that Ben had continued to disregard it. That's the kind of thing that wrecks a company. It can't be tolerated without damage."

"So if he couldn't solve it and couldn't tolerate it, what did he do?"

"He took two steps. George talked to him on the phone and said the expenditures were to be discontinued immediately. Again, Ben was compliant and gracious. A month passed, and the expenditures continued. George phoned again, saying he was coming to London and wanted a meeting in Ben's office at 9:00 on the fifth. George was there at 9:00; Ben arrived at 9:30. George let him know this was but a small example of the continuous disrespect and that he wanted Ben's resignation immediately."

"Was that the end of it?"

"No," said Andy. "An interesting and unanticipated result occurred. Through an informal channel, unknown to George, Ben arranged to address the Board of Directors the next week."

"Did George permit this to happen?"

"He did, but only after he had met with the Board to review the situation and to confirm the requested resignation. He pointed out that it was an example of insubordination, that he could not be effective as chief executive officer if it were to be tolerated, and that the termination which had been arranged must be final or he would not remain in the chief executive post."

"And then?"

"Ben met with the Board, made a dramatic presentation of his history with the company, what he saw as its future, thanked them, and left. His resignation was accepted. That was the end of it as far as George was concerned, but, of course, it sent a message throughout the company. Our days of bureaucratic live-and-let-live were over.

"I've told you this story in sufficient depth so you can see George's concept of conflict resolution. Conflict is close to inevitable but is not harmful in itself. His intention was to dig into this situation and get it back on a sound footing, but the plan didn't work. He had to put up with a bad situation or bring it to an end. He took the better course.

"The gain is that it clears the decks for future action. The difficulty is that it may cause people in the organization to say, 'That's what you get for advocacy,' because they fail to realize that the issue is not one of advocacy but one of Ben's resisting the development of a sound working relationship with George and with others as well. Such misunderstandings are a danger, and can lead to the accusation of executive high-handedness. Furthermore, a chief executive can't, in good conscience, make the facts clear so that everyone understands why he did what he did. It is unwise for any executive to voice public criticism of any other executive. At best it is dishonest, and at worst, is self-serving."

"Well, this has something of the character of a Greek drama. How would you describe George's approach to decision making?"

"Well, to be frank about it, he has deep doubts about unilateral decision making. He knows it's commonly said that someone has to make decisions and that the top man, in the final analysis, can't involve others in all of them. He believes this. But George says he, at least for one, does not have a large enough head to supply himself with the necessary perspectives without getting the thoughts of others. He has no difficulty making up his mind. What helps make up his mind is deliberation. I think that's a key to understanding how this company is operating."

"What does that mean with regard to delegation?"

"That's a good question. In areas where policy has been made official, he expects subordinates to act without consultation. However, he expects them to deliberate their decisions with others. Given that proviso, they are autonomous, and for them to come to him for discussion or approval would waste their time and his as well. However, he does sit with subordinates and review their operations from time to time. He does so primarily to keep posted, though such reviews also involve a critique that subordinates find genuinely beneficial. Once a review and critique session has been completed, he backs subordinates to the limit. This is an important way he has strengthened operation of the company, but it can't be understood independently of other aspects."

"How does he deal with delegation when guidelines are unclear?"

"He expects subordinates to touch base. This is a reverse delegation in which the initiative comes from below. Whenever a matter is complex or in a significant gray area or when guidelines are insufficient for the person in authority to see broader implications, deliberation is again critical. If the problem is within the subordinate's domain and has no significant implications for effectiveness beyond that particular operation, then, after deliberation, it is the subordinate's decision to make. When the issue is in a gray area or bears on the operation of the rest of the company or some significant component, then George takes an intermediate step. He frequently arranges group sessions so that each person whose operations are likely to be affected has an opportunity to get involved and to reach agreement regarding the course of action. Were the issue a truly major one for which George alone shoulders responsibility, he would be the ultimate decision maker for the larger interest, but still only after extensive deliberation which already had led to implicit understanding and agreement."

"What about meetings of the major people who report to him?" asked Walt.

"That's where much of the decision making takes place, sometimes during the session itself. But more often than not, he returns to his office and writes the decision out in longhand in a calendar diary. He makes it a matter of record. He says that writing the decision is better than giving it to a secretary or dictating it because he can ponder it and crystallize in his mind the next steps that will follow from it. His calendar provides notes that can be reexamined to assess the wisdom of having made the decision that way."

"Even though the topic may not bear directly on the responsibilities of several of the subordinates?"

"Yes, often under those conditions. You might see this as wasteful. From his standpoint, however, there is a reason for it. It's part of executive development. He wants every executive to have not only a specialist but a generalist point of view, not only subsidiary or divisional knowledge but a corporate orientation, to be able to assess what is in the larger interest from a divisional or subsidiary perspective and also from a corporate perspective. Another issue becomes visible. Part of the reason for deliberation is to find the best solution for complex problems. He finds pooled thinking indispensable. The other part of the reason is to educate and to ensure maximum gain for future executive competence."

"How often does the top group meet?"

"We have regularly scheduled meetings once a week, usually on Monday mornings. Sometimes they last through lunch. Sometimes we have special meetings, and throughout the day there are touch-base sessions. While George believes that deliberation is the safest way to make complex decisions, he also believes that delegation is an excellent way to mobilize the energies of others as long as clear guidelines geared to the corporate whole are in place."

"A final area is the use of critique as a learning tool. How would you picture George's use of critique?"

"We have routinely stepped back from problems to test whether our approach is as sound as it might be, and if not, how it might be made sounder by involving other people, gathering more data, or talking outside the company. One method is his calendar diary. Another is the routine review of subordinates' delegated decisions.

"I don't think I mentioned it, but he frequently spends the last thirty minutes of a larger conference initiating a discussion of how well members interacted. Were there impediments to openness and frankness? If so, what were they? Did anyone feel cut off or blocked in expressing concerns fully? How were reservations and doubts dealt with? Did anyone withhold opinions to avoid getting hopped on? How might the quality of discussion be improved?

"This isn't ritualized, and it's not programmed; but it occurs often enough to keep George alert to how well discussions take place."

"One more question occurs to me that I'd like to pose before we quit."

"What's that?"

"It's a deep question, and I will understand if you think it not appropriate, but it's a matter of curiosity to me. He has had the chief executive position for ten years. He's forty-eight. Retirement age is sixty-five. What happens between now and then? Does he have political aspirations or retirement plans?"

"It's an appropriate enough question," said Andy, "but not necessarily a snap to answer. He's never had political ambitions, but on the other hand he feels that industry is or should be a training ground for civic leadership. I don't mean business people running segments of the government; that has been reasonably successful. However, the White House leadership has never come from presidents who might be regarded as professional leaders. All you have to do to see that is to track history in the twentieth century.

"I've heard him say, 'I'm not clear in my own mind as to why the American presidency has never been held by a person with an established record of leadership in the business world. Perhaps, if the public views business and politics as opposite ends of a continuum, a business leader as president is unlikely, but I wouldn't rule it out.' George knows he can look forward to excellent prospects for this company during the period of his tenure. He says, 'The only thing I don't look forward to is retirement.' "

"This has been a comprehensive examination of executive leadership," Walt said as the interview concluded. "I have talked with many at the pinnacle of executive life, and George is one who comprehends the issues involved in exercising leadership effectively."

SUMMARY

The 9,9 style of leadership describes a positive connection between organizational needs for production and the needs of people for full and rewarding work experiences. The leader's desire is to contribute to corporate success by involving others so that they too may contribute. A can-do spirit is contagious; it inspires a win attitude in others and promotes enthusiasm, voluntarism, spontaneity, and openness.

Motivations

The positive motivation of a 9,9-oriented leader is contribution to the larger interest in the sense of genuine desire to help others reach their highest potential. The 9,9 achievement motivation comes from developing the competence required to make a positive contribution to the company and therefore pursue corporate goals and objectives with the same enthusiasm as if they were one's own.

The 9,9-oriented leader seeks to avoid advancing selfish interests at the expense of the larger interests of the corporation. This motivation may be termed enlightened self-interest or altruistic egotism, because it often does result in personal gain.

Initiative

George displayed initiative which had the effect of creating involvement of others. The result was that others followed his example and also exercised initiative. An example cited was the promotion system conversion from seniority to merit. Rather than effecting this change by edict, George worked with others to ensure their involvement and commitment.

The Grid statement of 9,9 initiative is: "I exert vigorous effort, and others join in enthusiastically."

Inquiry

The word *thoroughness* is characteristic of George's inquiry. He made an ongoing study of the organization. He was an avid reader of business publications, along with internal documents, and studied people as well. He had concern that others be informed beyond their specialties and he made a special effort to obtain firsthand information through visits to outside locations.

The Grid statement of 9,9 inquiry is: "I search for and validate information. I invite and listen for opinions, attitudes, and ideas different than my own. I continually reevaluate the soundness of my own and others' facts, beliefs, and positions."

Advocacy

George had strong convictions based on deep understanding of issues and communicated them with candor. He expected the same of others in order that he could consider the full range of issues, including reservations, doubts, and disagreements, before taking an action. His knowledge and encouragement of others to speak out in the interest of the organization allowed such capacity to contribute to corporate benefit.

The Grid statement of 9,9 advocacy is: "I feel it is important to express my concerns and convictions. I respond to ideas sounder than my own by changing my mind."

Conflict Solving

George's approach to conflict was to dig into underlying causes and then work to bring about resolution. When necessary, as was the case with Ben, he first established the facts of the situation and worked to resolve the problem. In the end he was forced to take decisive action. He saw conflict as inevitable but not necessarily bad, as it provided the opportunity to examine many sides of an issue. Another tactic he used in dealing with conflict was to set the immediate disagreement aside and look at the problem from an ideal perspective. This tactic provided opportunity to study the actual situation in a more objective fashion.

The Grid statement of 9,9 conflict solving is: "When conflict arises, I seek out reasons for it in order to resolve underlying causes."

Decision Making

George took responsibility for decisions on a unilateral basis when appropriate but with deliberation beforehand. Depending upon the issue, he involved as many others as appropriate to contribute to the decision, partly to gain their involvement and commitment. In areas where operational policy was established, subordinates were autonomous, although expected to deliberate their decisions with others. Through review and critique sessions he kept himself aware of operations and able to provide help to subordinates. He also involved others in decisions as a matter of education and development where appropriate.

The Grid statement of 9,9 decision making is: "I place high value on arriving at sound decisions. I seek understanding and agreement."

Critique

George used critique extensively as a learning tool. He reexamined operational decisions by routine critiques of delegated decisions, by gathering additional data, by going outside the company, and by involving other people. In addition, ongoing critique tested the soundness of interaction during meetings.

The Grid statement of 9,9 critique is: "I encourage two-way examination of how we do things and work together with others in order to strengthen operations by learning how to get better results."

Overview of the 9,9 Grid Style

The attitudes illustrated by Thomas are useful in characterizing the underlying thinking of any 9,9-oriented executive. The specific episodes that reveal these attitudes can always be expected to be unique. The reason is that the content issues vary greatly from corporation to corporation. The content concerns of a chief executive in a bank are likely to be significantly different from those of the chief executive in an oil company, or a high technology organization, or a company involved in trading commodities. The process aspects of leadership underlie the content issues, and a 9,9-oriented leader effectively utilizes human resources in solving complex problems, regardless of the content.

"A prince of a person," or a "star" might be shorthand ways of identifying a 9,9-oriented executive; a prince or a star may lead an old company or a new one, a heavy industry concern or a high technology corporation, an investment house or a brokerage firm.

Chapter 11 reports how another 9,9-oriented chief executive exercised leadership in a different set of circumstances. The reader may be interested in skipping to that chapter in order to get a feel for how unimportant these surface differences are, relative to the basic orientation.

Top leadership leaves its impact on the bottom line partly by the culture that it creates. When 9,9 values have become widespread throughout a corporate culture, they become evident in many different management practices.

At least three explanations can be offered for the observation that top leadership is one of the strongest influences in shaping corporate culture. First, the leader's thoughts and actions establish precedents and signal that "This is okay, but not that." In time, these established practices and attitudes become a part of the culture.

Secondly, because of the powerful desire of people to be accepted by their colleagues and peers, the tendency to conform is a significant influence which undoubtedly operates under all Grid styles.[1]

Thirdly, subordinates often model themselves on their leader's behavior. The adage "birds of a feather" is a more reliable guide than "opposites attract" for understanding personnel choice and selection. When leaders select and promote others like themselves, they further imprint their styles on the organization.

REFERENCES

1. Robert R. Blake and Jane S. Mouton. *Productivity: The Human Side*, AMACOM, New York, 1981.

WORKING HARDER OR SMARTER?

"Larry Askew was a brilliant financial analyst," said Bill Jenkins. "As an outside consultant, he'd done a whale of a job in developing a strategic plan to guide the company through the next decade. It was a natural for the Board of Directors, who approved his plan at about the time his predecessor was leaving, to say, 'Who could do it better than the person who designed it?' So they gave him the nod."

"So why don't we begin there?" asked Walt.

"Whatever else you can say, Larry put out the effort," said Bill, who had been one of three executive vice presidents under Larry. "You can't fault him for that. No one ever tried harder or worked more hours."

"I sense a note of reservation. What was his problem?"

"I'd describe him as rigid, unbending. Once his mind was made up on a course of action, that was it. He overlooked evidence that his course of action wasn't working and plowed forward."

"What drove him?"

"He was a working machine. His motto was 'Work is the ultimate opportunity,' and he took full measure of that opportunity, the eighteen-hours-a-day, seven-days-a-week sort of thing."

"What did he spend his time doing?"

"He took problems apart, down to the last detail. Nothing was too small to escape notice. Only when he had crossed the last t did he feel secure in the actions he authorized," said Bill. "But working on the details was just the surface side of the problem."

"How come?"

"It worked this way. He didn't just sit behind his desk and wait for problems to come to him. When they weren't coming, he'd go out to find them. There was a great tendency during his regime for turmoil to follow his footsteps as he kept top executives busy feeding his voracious appetite for detail.

"I remember one time this happened. He was studying a technical report on sales trends in the Pacific region. Some numbers didn't add up to 100. The mistake shook his confidence in what he was reading, and he began to question the whole presentation. All hell broke loose. He was on the phone in no time, trying to learn who had prepared the report, what sources of data had been used, and who had verified the figures, if anyone.

"The trouble is—while he was zealous about the numbers and verified the addition and subtraction—he failed to dig into the greater complexities of the issues behind them. When a downtrend was evident, he saw it as something that had to be turned around. He didn't relate it to product obsolescence, to the headquarters' tendency to strangle the advertising budget, or to the salary structure's being below area competition, which constantly drained the company of good people."

"He failed to see the forest for the trees?"

"That's my reading of it. He was drawn to facts, figures, and concrete evidence like a dog tracking a scent. This had a tendency to get him working on the wrong problem.

"In a certain way, details gave Larry tunnel vision. Because of his mastery of detail, he did, in effect, control situations and dominate everyone, but never in a hostile manner. He drove himself and others, but on the other hand he assumed they were as determined to make the corporation a success as he. He adopted the motto of Henry Ford II: 'Never explain, never complain.' He didn't complain, nor did he engage in shallow discussion. It was all work and no play all the way.

"When the company experienced a financial downturn, this drove him all the harder to get numbers to learn more about what was going on in order to fix it. It's not easy to turn such a situation around. The inability to reverse a trend seemed to him a close cousin to the word 'failure.' As the problems became chronic, he worked all the harder to get out of them. That's another reason he got to the extended hours and seven-days-a-week schedule.

"In walking around headquarters, he usually had a negative, who-did-it attitude. People felt threatened by him, and few felt brave enough to stand up to him. The best ones seemed to find better jobs elsewhere, and those who stayed and resisted were felled by his ax, one by one. Even the secretaries trembled, I think, and junior managers occasionally signaled to one another that they had just had contact with the big boss."

"Even though people gave him the yes-sir treatment or tried to back off, conflicts must have arisen. How did he deal with them?"

"Let me give you an example. One time the marketing people scheduled an appointment to get his okay on a new product line. Marketing had done a thorough study because they knew he was a hard guy to get something past. They had done market surveys of customer interest; they had selected a plant where the manufacturing could be undertaken without further significant investment in equipment; they had developed a pricing strategy to recoup developmental costs in two years. The presentation was spirited. As they got into it, they stimulated one another and became more and more enthusiastic. This was possible because Larry had the tendency to sit quietly by and listen until people had finished their presentations. Usually at that point he began to interrogate, but on this occasion his initial response was, 'I'm sorry, gentlemen. Now is not the right time.'

"The marketing people were flabbergasted. They had expected to be questioned, but they also expected approval, since they were so convinced of the soundness of the new line. After a pause, they began one by one to reiterate the advantages of introducing the line. Larry shrugged his shoulders, threw his hands in front of him, cocked his head, and said, 'That's the way it's going to be.'

"Later on they found that Larry thought the new product idea was okay but he had nixed it because of a cash flow problem. If he had told them that, they might have addressed the matter of timing or scheduling, but he wasn't one to reveal his mind. You know—'never explain, never complain.'

"Since he did not agree, they had no recourse. The suppression had been successful. Sure, the disagreement disappeared, but the marketing people were mystified and retained convictions about the validity of their proposition. They knew there was no further basis to continue. It simply would not be acceptable to continue. Nothing to do but cave in. Even though Larry had cut them off without apparent anger or hostility, they resented it.

"You can see what this approach does to subordinates. The marketing department had gone all-out to establish a real position in a new market that could also make a positive profit difference; they had done so in a creative manner. But Larry cut them off at the pass—no way they could go forward. So what do they do? You know the old phrases: 'hide in the bushes,' 'don't go out on a limb,' 'let the old man stew in his own juice.' It's a case where 'strong' leadership almost produced corporate death."

"Was he an action-oriented person?"

"Very high," said Bill. "A total leader, with no reluctance to move. When he saw people going in a wrong direction, he didn't hesitate to turn them around by saying, 'I'd like to have you do it this way' or 'Do it this way,' which sent the message, 'Don't argue with me.' His responsibility was to concentrate on what he saw to be important. He never let go.

"Time after time, I've seen his card-file memory work. He'd be with somebody who'd been involved in a problem at an earlier time. He'd shift the topic and say, 'Six months ago we were shipping 10,000 units; we had an order backlog of double that amount.' You'd say, 'We cleared $13 per unit.' Then he'd say, 'What's the status of that today? What's preventing further progress? Can we move it along faster?' His persistence led everyone to know that once they'd been identified with a problem they would always come to his attention until they'd dealt with it to his satisfaction, and even then he kept it 'on file.' He was not a start-and-stop type of guy. Had the memory of an elephant."

"You said he was a great believer in taking action. Does that mean any sort of action?"

"No, I can't say that. What determined his views on problems was whether he could amass a set of facts. He tended to ignore or brush aside problems that were not documented. Facts defined problems rather than problems defining the need for facts. He didn't like guesswork and he didn't trust intuition. There was no such thing as 'feel.' One of his favorite questions was, 'What are the facts?' So he placed attention on numbers. We probably have the most sophisticated control and information systems in the industry. He was always watching the pennies. This was one area where no expense was spared."

"Did he consult when deciding on priorities?"

"Rarely. He set priorities himself. He let deputies know where he was concentrating his next effort just as he was about to get into it. They were often caught in the dark. He would send for me or ask my secretary to make an appointment, but it was not his custom to say, 'Mary, I want to talk about problem X with Bill.' Being unable to read his mind, I would walk into his office in a state of ignorance. This was his typical way. You might say he was a self-contained leader."

"What we've discussed suggests he was a practical person. Did he also have a philosophical outlook?" asked Walt.

"He had a philosophical position related to free enterprise: the role of the individual is what makes the difference. He was a strong believer in that. That was the building block of his concept of leadership and organization. Many activities reflected that outlook in terms of promotion and reward, training and development, and so on.

"I've frequently heard him say, 'My approach to advancement is "sink or swim." Employ technically competent people and give them an opportunity to prove themselves.' Equality of opportunity meant equal opportunity to sink. Selecting 'good people' meant focusing on technical aspects of the job. If a person had a good knowledge and skill base, particularly in the financial aspects of the job, then Larry felt a person needed only leg room to prove himself or herself. The cream will rise to the top.

"In the long run this approach made a contribution to corporate decay. The development of managerial skills received little or no attention. There was always pressure for production, but the negative effects were ignored. Couple this with Larry's tendency to surround himself with yes-men, and you end up with no managerial talent in the middle levels to feed into executive positions. No one person can do all the thinking for a corporation this size.

"He felt he was exercising strong leadership only when he was totally on top of a problem, without help, assistance, or support from anyone. That expressed his concept of a leader's responsibility for guiding the corporation: every leader responsible for managing himself, and no one depending on others. Trouble is—he saw subordinates not as yea-sayers but as savvy people when they saluted his wish. Those who argued or got into conflict with him were 'bullheaded.' The fact is, he was a poor reader of human character and competence."

"How did others react to this?"

"It was one of the more unfortunate aspects of his leadership, partly because he didn't project a vision of the organization. He didn't lift people's aspirations or hopes or excite them with challenges. He saw feelings and emotions as barriers to rational thinking. That's why he rarely expressed anger and hostility. If he felt them, he didn't show them. It was the real-men-don't-cry attitude. We would have been a happier and more successful company if he had not been so contained."

"The picture coming through is of a solo operator."

"That's a bit strong, but in a way he was the computer user, and everyone else was either a programmer or a chip. Authority was centralized in him, and the rest of the organization served his needs for information. On one occasion when I was heading up the British operation, he asked me to come to New York on an urgent basis. As I now know, he called two executive vice presidents and a couple of others to New York about the same time. He gave each of us a fact-gathering assignment to be carried out in our market areas. He wanted us to report on the trends of national economies, governmental expenditures, interest rates, predicted currency fluctuations, and patterns of private spending, with the request that we back up our conclusions with statistical studies wherever possible. With each of us contributing to an overall European view, it could have been a terrific joint effort. If he had given us these assignments as a team, we could have worked out a joint strategy. But he didn't. He spoke to each one of us in private and made it clear that we were not to tell the others. The secrecy separated subordinates who could have given one another mutual support. It came through as a blind spot," said Bill.

"How would you explain it?"

"If he had all the facts flowing into him from the different locations, then he could put together the grand strategy. It put him in a position to see how the various companies in Europe might work with one another, without any one of us having a broad enough basis of knowledge to challenge him. This put him in control. It permitted him to make decisions based on extensive data, and it avoided the eruption of conflict about the strategy."

"Would he see this as one-alone decision making?"

"No, he'd see it as splendid teamwork."

"Would you see it as sound teamwork?"

"Not a chance," replied Bill. "Larry removed the possibility of teamwork by the way he gave the assignment.

"It's the same path he took for the financial study that got him the presidential nod five years ago. The Board of Directors failed to see the implication. They said, 'He put it together; he understands it; he should implement it.'

"The problem started with implementation," Bill continued.

"How did it?"

"Larry didn't have firsthand knowledge about the real field situation. He had information collected for him which he put together. The information suppliers didn't know the complex thinking that went into the planning. They fed data to Larry, but this gave them no particular insight as to what the Board had authorized. Their foot-dragging made it difficult to translate the overall plan into action in the local field situation. It hasn't been put in place yet. That's one of my main jobs—to develop a plan for securing and strengthening our market position and getting an earnings trend under way.

"Larry saw subordinates as extensions of himself, merely as executors of activities, conceived by him, that they didn't understand. He was an over-delegator.

"Since he eliminated teamwork, the implementation process could not benefit from deliberated decisions. His domination prevented deliberation, and without deliberation it just wasn't possible to put a plan into effect."

"Why do you think he did that?"

"I think he feared a team or a group. If my analysis is correct, he prevented us from operating as a team. He felt people lose their capacity for independence of thought and judgment in a group and can be readily swayed. He may also have figured there is strength in numbers and feared that together we might resist him in a manner impossible for a single individual."

"What about the role of performance appraisal?"

"Nonexistent. He seemed to dread feedback. Too personal, I suspect. Feedback might communicate feelings. Larry thought that emotions had no place in business. He disregarded performance appraisal. That's what sink-or-swim is all about: you don't have to tell a subordinate he is drowning. Larry wasn't uncertain himself, and he didn't like conversations with others that led to uncertainty, tentativeness, or even the exploration of possibilities. He'd button up his reactions, and no one knew what they were until he'd explode. He liked definiteness—black-and-white, yes-and-no situations."

"I expect that his use of critique—you know, studying a project to learn from it—was impoverished as well."

"It was absent, and probably for the same reasons. Reluctance to deal with feelings prevented him from handling what I believe to be critical factors in successful management. This was an unfortunate aspect of Larry's leadership. However, my points of view are not what we're talking about, so I'll stop at that."

"How much did Larry change during the years you knew him?"

"I don't think he learned much at all, and it's because he stayed away from feedback and critique. He did change by putting out more and more effort—the eighteen-hours-a-day thing—but this change was due to fear of failure. His retirement was requested by the Board, but he didn't go out in a blaze of glory. It was a godsend for the corporation."

"Why do you think you got the nod as Larry's replacement instead of an outsider or one of the other chief executives—or even some other person who may have been a dark horse?"

"I can fill you in on my background, and then you can be the judge of that. I've made my career in this company. I've rotated through the various divisions, functions, and locations. Before coming here, I'd been managing director of our largest subsidiary in Europe. Our headquarters was just on the north side of London. For all practical purposes, Larry had been calling the shots 'heard round the world' from New York. I replaced one of his selections, about whom it was said that 'whenever New York sneezes, the willows bend on the Thames.' Larry was a bulldog and he went for yes-men. But they only survived as long as things went well. I turned the situation around in London, and that may have led the Board to feel I might be able to do it again. I suspect I got the nod because of my broad corporate knowledge, and because I wasn't one of Larry's boys."

"Well, I'll be back in five years to get the next installment!"

"Fair enough. I'll look forward to that."

SUMMARY

The 9,1 leadership style rests on the assumption that there is an inherent contradiction between the organization's needs for productivity and the human needs of its members. This means production objectives can be met only by controlling and directing in a way that compels compliance. The logical extension of this assumption is to arrange conditions of work in ways that diminish subordinates' needs for exercising independent thought and judgment. Such controls surface in the forms of cost centers, budgets, and other methods of keeping tabs on operations. Data gathering substitutes for thinking, analysis, and judgment.

Motivations

Viewing subordinates as extensions of himself, Larry dealt with them one-on-one rather than as a team, because he feared their strength as a group. A key to recognizing the 9,1 leadership style is its self-emphasis: "I alone am in charge, I know how things should be done, and I am responsible for success. Lack of success is due to factors beyond my control." When in control Larry felt a sense of strength, power, and freedom from reliance on others. To depend on others indicated weakness.

The negative motivation in this type of leadership is fear of failure. Losing control signals defeat. As the downtrend became apparent, Larry suffered personal misery. His response to the downtrend was putting out more and more effort, rather than working smarter, and thus the downtrend continued.

Initiative

The more difficulties Larry encountered the harder he worked. Initiatives were self-determined; he did not permit others to contribute. Rather than waiting for problems to surface he searched for them, which had the effect of keeping things in turmoil.

The 9,1 initiative statement is: "I drive myself and others."

Inquiry

Larry inquired intently, studying reports and documents as well as assigning others to bring him data, numbers, and facts. He then neatly catalogued all such information in his card-file mind. One of his favorite phrases was "What are the facts?" Numbers represented a higher order of importance than the deeper issues behind them. As a result he lacked vision and was unable to see trends and general issues—in other words, unable to see the forest for the trees.

The 9,1 inquiry statement is: "I investigate facts, beliefs, and positions so that I am in control of any situation and to assure myself that others are not making mistakes."

Advocacy

Larry had convictions about free enterprise and the role of the individual. To him, equality of opportunity meant only an equal chance at the start. Individualism took over at that point. His motto was "sink or swim." Much of his concept of organization, how to structure it, and how to develop it came from these notions. He held strong convictions in a black-and-white, close-minded way. There were no exceptions, and he was intolerant of challenge to his beliefs.

The 9,1 advocacy statement is: "I stand up for my opinions, attitudes, and ideas even though it means rejecting others' views."

Conflict Solving

Larry anticipated and avoided conflict by thorough preparation. When disagreement persisted or resistance continued, he withdrew from further discussion and adopted the take-it-or-leave-it attitude exemplified by his reaction to the marketing proposal. Since it was an unrealistic option to leave it, subordinates had little choice but to take it. He prevented teamwork partly because he felt people would be able to resist more effectively in a group setting.

The 9,1 conflict-solving statement is: "When conflict arises I try to cut it off or win my position."

Decision Making

The leader had to be on top of everything with minimum help from others. Decisions came from within and had a unilateral character leading to centralized organization structure with large and small decisions going up to be finalized. His idea of teamwork was to employ subordinates to do research independently of one another. As the recipient of all the facts, he made the decision and saw that others implemented it.

The 9,1 decision-making statement is: "I place high value on making my own decisions and am rarely influenced by others."

Critique

Larry did not use feedback, performance appraisal, or critique. His concept of "rational man" prohibited feelings from intruding into business decisions. He lost opportunities for learning and development. His sink-or-swim outlook meant "You don't need to tell a man he's drowning." Those who could have given accurate feedback were unwilling to do so. They became "yes men," further encumbering his ability to correlate his mass of facts with real-world problems.

The 9,1 critique statement is: "I pinpoint others' weaknesses or failure to measure up."

Adverse Consequences

Larry's omissions bring into perspective some of the hazards he faced in dealing with subordinates.

> Larry turned down the marketing proposal submitted
> by subordinates without providing any rationale for
> his decision (pp. 43–44).

What are the likely consequences of this kind of behavior for any leader? When diligent effort on a proposal nets a flat rejection, subordinates learn only that the proposal is unacceptable. Unless the leader provides a clear explanation of the reasons for the rejection, he or she sacrifices any gains from a critique of the proposal's limitations. Subordinates lose insights they might utilize in preparing future proposals.

The leader also pays the price of lost motivation. Subordinates ask, "What's the use of investing all that energy just to get turned down?" They also learn that the way to get approval on a proposal is to find out what the boss wants and give it to him. "You've got to play him like a violin," they conclude.

When the leader provides a rationale behind a rejection, and even better, when a full discussion leads to understanding and agreement, the company gains a development objective along with increased commitment to the decision.

> Larry requested meetings with subordinates, without
> telling them what he wanted to discuss (p. 44).

Subordinates are likely to come to such a meeting either without involvement ("Here we go again") or with an uneasy feeling, not knowing if the boss is sitting on a time bomb, about to drop the other shoe, or what. Without knowing the purpose of a meeting, attendees are unable to prepare and, at best, can contribute only what they already know. With the opportunity to ponder a specific issue beforehand, subordinates can prepare themselves to contribute to the purpose of the meeting and thus enhance significantly the quality of discussion.

> Larry asked several subordinates to collect data for
> him on the same problem independently and without
> consultation with each other (pp. 46–47).

The practice of getting information from subordinates is all to the good. In truth, the leader gains the benefit of having others do what he is either unprepared or unable to do by virtue of other requirements.

What is potentially sacrificed by this approach? Subordinates may not be informed why the multiple assignment strategy is being utilized. If they discover that others are studying the same problem, they become suspicious either of the boss or of one another. Suspicion of the boss can produce collusion. The subordinates may agree to give the leader approximately the same answers.

Subordinates' suspicion of one another may lead to destructive competition, as each tries to outdo or outsmart the others rather than placing primary focus on their tasks. When subordinates are discouraged from collaborating with one another, there is no possibility of synergy. Individual tasks cannot add up to a coherent whole. Exploration for gaps in information cannot continue.

Subordinates learn that the boss does not trust them to carry out assignments in a mutually cooperative way. A leader should solve a problem of insufficient mutual cooperation by developing the spirit of collaboration and/or the necessary skills for subordinates to operate autonomously as well as interdependently to the end result of corporate gain.

> Larry formulated a strategic marketing plan for the
> company based on data collected by others. He had
> no firsthand knowledge of the data nor did he use
> subordinates to assess the plan and its implementa-
> tion (pp. 46–47).

One drawback to this kind of one-alone decision making is that the leader cannot benefit from hearing the plan discussed by its developers or, later, by its implementers. The implementers are more likely to know the details of operations and to be able to test a plan. If a plan is not successful, the leader learns from them what needs to be changed—the plan or the operations.

A longer-term, more hidden consequence of keeping subordinates in the dark is to put them in a weaker position to implement a plan as rapidly and fully as might otherwise be possible if they had full understanding of the background thinking and the objectives. The corollary is also true; not seeing the sense of a plan, subordinates drag their feet.

Overview of the 9,1 Grid Style

Different executives operating from the 9,1 orientation show various features of leadership, but all are variations on the basic theme. Some are exacting taskmasters who know what is best, whose actions and concerns are focused on one thought: getting results. Their mental gyroscopes maintain a single direction.

Sometimes anger and hostility are outstanding features. "Looking for a fight," "going on the warpath," "having a short fuse," or a "chip on his shoulder" are common descriptions of the executive who feels, "I've found I can't get anything worthwhile without fighting for it." The executive may be so involved in controlling production that he or she runs roughshod over others.

A 9,1-oriented executive's sense of strength comes from feeling able to overcome hurdles and remove obstacles. An inflexible determination to control, to plow ahead, crack the whip, and say, "Do it or else," is typical. To solicit suggestions, recommendations, advice, or guidance seems to such an executive an indication of weakness or incompetence.

For still other 9,1-oriented executives, the greatest dread is to falter, defeated. When failure occurs, mastery, control, and domination have broken down. They place blame on colleagues and subordinates, think-ing, "Next time I'll watch them more closely." A 9,1-oriented executive feels, "I am the reason for my successes; failure is caused by the actions of others. Never trust them."

SUGGESTIONS FOR CHANGE

Below are suggestions for change that a 9,1-oriented leader might want to consider.

Motivation

1. If subordinates think it wise either to salute or to stay out of your way, increase their involvement by getting them to open up and participate in solving problems. Utilize subordinates as resources who can contribute more to the decisions.
2. Try to prevent fear of failure from causing you to hold information inside yourself; this keeps people from acting until told what to do.

Initiative

1. Get others to take initiative in situations where previously you have called the shots.
2. When you see a needed action, you immediately move to fill the void. Diagnose why others don't act when the need is obvious. Aid them to do so.
3. Check out whether you could get better results by consulting your subordinates and colleagues. You may be underconsulting and not taking advantage of support that is available.

Inquiry

1. If you don't consult others, you may be depriving yourself of information important for doing a better job.
2. Don't discount information that comes from sources you dislike. Remember that IQ is independent of Grid style.
3. By not listening, you may be cutting off information needed for sound solutions.

Advocacy

1. Get others to speak before stating your own position.
2. Ask others to react to your position rather than demanding they accept it as final.
3. When others are advocating a position, find out what they really mean rather than mentally rehearsing counterarguments.
4. When advocating a position, you can help others if you express any reservations about it that you have.

Conflict

1. If differences of opinion end in a fight, take a closer look at your own reasons for arguing.
2. Listen to others' points of view before automatically telling them why they're wrong. Their thinking and analysis may be at least as good as your own.
3. Suppressing differences doesn't eliminate them, but does increase resentment and limits your ability to exercise effective leadership.

Decisions

1. Slow down decision making. Consult with others. Take reservations or disagreements into account, or at least explain why you cannot.
2. Communicate the rationale behind decisions you've made on an individual basis.

Critique

1. Feedback can be objective when it describes what you observe others doing. Critique does not have to be blame-inducing or fault-finding.
2. Feedback should be a two-way street. Others may be able to contribute to your effectiveness if you allow them to tell you what they think and why.

6

NICE GUYS
FINISH
ALMOST LAST

"I've been having a series of discussions with members of the Board," said Walt Burton, "but I've not spent much time with Mankoff yet. Stanley thought it might be helpful to get your angle on how he's leading the company and then to get reactions from Lee Randolph before he and I talk."

"Well, I'd be glad to give you whatever I'm able to fill in," Will said, "but I don't know exactly what you want to know."

"Let me ask how long you have had this position and what your range of activities is."

"Well," began Will, "I've been in this job six years. I'm between a 'go-fer' and an aide-de-camp. Stanley makes a number of speeches and I help him. I draft the descriptive parts of the annual report. I often write letters for his signature. If there's a technical study he wants, I do that. Also I accompany him on trips and sit in on meetings to make notes on what has happened and review the approvals given or agreements made.

"I intended to take this job for a couple of years, but one thing has led to another. I keep on partly because I enjoy it, and also because it's an excellent window to how corporations are run."

"Do you see yourself as his confidant?"

"I think I'd better ask you to be more precise. What would a confidant be?"

"A confidant is a person with whom another person—like Stanley in this situation—is completely free and candid and with whom he or she feels comfortable in expressing criticism of others because he knows it will go no further. The leader feels secure in accepting information the subordinate is ready to provide. It's a relationship of complete trust, I might say, in which the confidant serves as an extension of the chief executive."

"The answer is no. My relationship is based on pure friendliness. I like him, and I think he likes me. I don't see it as my role to be anything but a faithful friend who brings him no misery, gives him no lectures, and offers no advice. With me, he can let his hair down and get things off his chest."

"Okay, let's move on. What makes him tick?"

"First of all, he's a big city VIP," replied Will. "He finds time to serve in the broader community; for example, on the hospital board. He's on the Rotary program committee and the Chamber of Commerce committee that entertains representatives from new businesses looking over our area. That's important in a company like ours, and he enhances our reputation by being visible as a community servant. He keeps the Board posted on new developments that they might find personally or financially interesting.

"Another thing that might provide some insight is that he hates being alone. I don't know how many times, when someone has left his office, he has come out to say something like, 'Let's take a walk. I like to spend time walking around—keeping a finger on the pulse.' But he's not really after 'pulse.' He wants human contact. He loves to mingle. He's a gregarious man. Likes to put his arm on a person's shoulder and ask, 'How're things going?'

"Stanley is well-known and well-liked because he remembers everyone's name and has an uncanny recall for the little details of personal life that causes people to know he is interested in them. It's great for morale. The troops pick up his spirit and like to have him around. The real benefit is to Stanley, though. He likes all that reflected warmth."

"How often does he go walking like that?"

"Not often, because he has such a busy schedule. That's a real problem— time management. I don't know how many cassettes he's listened to on that topic, but he just can't keep on schedule. He's a flop when it comes to interviews or starting and stopping conferences on time. People are so pleased to get a chance to talk to the president that they think, since he doesn't stop them, he wants to hear more, and so they keep on talking. He can't say something like, 'I've got the main points. Thanks for dropping by. Let me know how things go,' and bring the conference to a close. One of the results is that people line up to see him. It's a joke. Anyone is able to figure out that a conference scheduled at 10:00 a.m. won't take place until at least 11:00. Later in the day the lag time gets even longer."

"Let's look at the other side, then. Are there people he dislikes?"

"Well, that can't be answered yes or no. For one thing, he's an optimist. He wants to see the best. But he does come to dislike some people."

"Which kind?"

"Those who disappoint him."

"Does he let them know?"

"Oh, no—the opposite. One day he said, 'One of the things I find most unpleasant about being president is that I feel obligated to be nice to people, even those who disappoint me.'

"In my view he bends backwards to be friendly to people I know he dislikes and to agree with whatever they want. It appears he is even more solicitous of those he dislikes or who disagree with him than those he likes or agrees with. You might say he courts his enemies and makes an effort to bring them around. I know he sometimes proposes a round of golf with someone he dislikes, or he invites that person to join a party being planned. He goes the extra mile to be friendly with enemies."

"What's the effect?"

"It wouldn't be so bad if he did not tell his real friends what his feelings are about his enemies. It gets him into trouble when he has to be nice to a person he dislikes in the presence of a friend who knows the score."

"Tell me more about Stanley's reactions to disagreement."

"That's an interesting area, because it tells something of how he leads. He tends to be easy and to yield a point rather than stirring up a hornet's nest. I don't know how many times I have been in his office after someone has made a request or a proposal he disagrees with. He fusses about it, but then says something like, 'They didn't justify the 10 percent increase in the advertising budget, but I let them go with it. Later on we'll study area sales and see who was right.' He rationalizes that the future will be the final judge of the other person's wisdom or lack of it."

"What happens when the facts prove he was right?" asked Walt.

"He loves it," replied Will. "But I get frustrated because he never goes back to say, 'Why didn't it work?' or 'That's what I figured would happen.' It may be a quirk, but he would rather see the corporation suffer, albeit in silence, than to say to them, 'See, I was right in the first place.'"

"Well, let me ask it in another way. What actions does he take when an unpleasant situation must be faced?"

"At times he becomes a bit devious; I don't think intentionally devious, but others may get that impression. This happens when he is asked for a ruling but in turn he asks third parties to carry out an action he doesn't want to be directly associated with. For example, I've seen him ask a senior VP to speak with the president of a subsidiary, saying he (Mankoff) has consulted with others and they think it would be advisable for this president to speak directly with another subsidiary president and come to an agreement on some matter in dispute. He diffuses responsibility by consulting with others, asking a senior VP to take care of it, and expecting subsidiary presidents to solve a dispute that they have brought to him. He does not take a position or decide.

"He doesn't like unpleasant news or decisions. I've seen him grapple with an unfavorable earnings estimate that had to be released. Even within an hour or two before the release, subordinates will have denied to reporters that there would be negative news. He simply did not want to pass the unpleasant information on, and as a result subordinates are often in the dark."

"How does he react when the chips are down?"

"Oh, he'll speak up when he has to stand for something, but his statement is not all that clear-cut. When a subordinate comes up with a proposal or a request with which Stanley agrees, then he has no difficulty in affirming that this is a sound approach. On the other hand, take the case where different subordinates come up with contradictory recommendations. If one is accepted, the other can't be. Sometimes, without seeing the contradiction, he has agreed with both sides at different times. This has created deep mires of conflict between opposing subordinates. Even then, though, he lets these conflicts rage on. That explains some of the difficulties of coordination, and occasionally has generated the idea that he is not consistent. It's not that he is inconsistent or a poor thinker, but that he sometimes goes out on a limb by advocating something he would not have accepted had he spent more time in thinking it through. Whenever he can let people know he is in agreement, it seems to give him a real sense of closeness and camaraderie."

"Does this mean he lacks courage?"

"Yes. He doesn't have the courage of his convictions. That's the fascinating thing about it. He has convictions, but he becomes tentative and unsure when there is disagreement. Then he holds back. One of the prices he pays for this is that schemers have been able to pull the wool over his eyes."

"How well does he get himself informed on various problems and issues and what others are proposing?"

"I'd say not too well. First of all, except for current events in business magazines like *Forbes* and *Business Week*, he does not read. He doesn't read management interest books like *Megatrends* or *In Search of Excellence*. And he certainly doesn't pore over technical studies or internally generated documents. That's where I come in handy. When it is important for him to know something about some kind of study or report, he hands it to me and asks me to brief it. After we talk it over he may request a memorandum with the gist of the main points covered. A page or so is more than enough."

"You said he loves to talk with people. Is that how he picks up information?"

"Not really. Of course, people may volunteer information, and he certainly listens. Otherwise, he doesn't focus discussion in any depth to learn what others really think. He rarely puts people on the spot by asking pointed questions. He thinks probing is interrogation and that others might see him as suspicious or skeptical. That makes him uneasy and unwilling to go to the mat to find out what's underneath it."

"What's the impact of this approach to learning on the growth and development of the corporation?"

"I may be speaking out of turn, but he is not as well-informed as he should be. He avoids coming to grips with the facts and this results in delay. Procrastination is his formula for not sticking out his neck. His pleasant, chuckling way of saying, 'I just haven't gotten around to that yet,' makes him feel all is well even when he adds, 'I promise to get to it next week.' He promises performance, but eventually people catch on to his problem of time management.

"This also helps explain why we've had some projects that might never have been launched had they been investigated in depth. The corporation might have avoided some pretty horrendous mistakes. When Stanley gives these projects his blessing, the Board and everyone else assumes he knows what he's doing. Of course, this is hindsight, but he's been burned, and as a result he procrastinates on some important issues.

"Don't let me lead you to think Stanley's a pushover, just saying yes to everything. When the chips are down and something that he does not understand must be approved, he is reluctant to move forward for fear of Board rejection. When some important proposals that he felt unable to endorse have come before him, he has probably saved the corporation a good many millions by not recommending them to the Board. Outright rejection would have killed these projects, but he prefers the slow death that comes from procrastination."

"I take it he's not a man of action."

"On a scale from active to passive," responded Will, "I'd put him on the low end. But that's not quite accurate either, because he does respond by asking others to take initiative. He responds warmly without regard for what they do. He's not threatened by subordinates' invading his territory and taking independent actions that otherwise he might be expected to authorize. He may be overly trusting. He has created a climate of approval by positive attitudes toward initiative-taking under delegation. This has led to some strong subsidiaries, but it has moved the corporation in the direction of a conglomerate without a common-thread strategy. What we've lost in synergy, we've gained in subsidiary entrepreneurship.

"But then the problem of jealousy arises because one subsidiary sees another entering its own product line or beginning to market competitively. This can produce a hell of a fight over vested interests. I've mentioned that Stanley's strong suit is not conflict solving. If he took more initiative on strategy and planning, many of these rivalries would disappear, and we could also capitalize on synergistic potentials for growth."

"But there must be times when he does exercise direct initiative."

"Well, of course, there are. First of all, he limits initiative to actions he regards as authorized by his job description. Of course, he doesn't have a written job description, but the Board has created structures for compensation, new ventures, and other projects, and whenever a Board committee is appointed, that fact automatically defines the activity as beyond his range of freedom. He does an excellent job of bringing to these Board committees whatever they request, and he occasionally brings them information of obvious relevance to their interests. But, in a certain sense, that is exercising responsibility rather than initiative.

"There are two kinds of situations where I have seen him take action that had an adverse quality. One is when his superiors request him to carry out an unpleasant assignment. Stanley doesn't hesitate to move when the Board is solidly behind him or when he is acting in its behalf. When these conditions prevail, he is strong and confident, even though the action may have the effect of hurting people. He feels no real sense of personal responsibility. It's not *him* doing something to *them*. In subtle ways, he lets those who are affected by his actions know that.

"He avoids taking personal initiative by hiding behind authority and by delegating jobs to put the onus on somebody else. By and large, the Board likes this because this gives it a lot of power.

"When acting in his own name, he becomes anxious and indecisive, and he procrastinates. Presidents of subsidiaries like it; it makes them more powerful."

"Does he work as a message passer?"

"No, he's not just a message passer. He adds something to the message. He communicates bad news with sympathy, compassion, and understanding. The recipient accepts it in good spirits. Members of the Board marvel at the low-key way he gets things done. But at the same time he avoids exposing himself to personal rejection."

"What impact does this approach have on his executive leadership? For example, how does he run meetings of his top group?"

"I happen to be secretary to the group, and attend all of its meetings. He calls it his executive committee. They get together one day a month to discuss the business. This is more a forum for exchange than for planning or decision making, though he also uses it to get action on matters of interest to the Board.

"Its members run over him. There is no coordination, or little in any event, and when it is provided, it's because some member feels a need to coordinate his efforts with someone else's rather than Mankoff's effort to ensure that nothing falls in the crack. I've seen members of his executive committee almost defy him, even somewhat arrogantly. I've already mentioned situations where insubordination occurred, and insubordination and defiance are close to blood kin. I've said to myself, and I've heard others say, that he needs to fire one of them on the spot to make an object lesson. But I don't see the prospect of that happening. He rationalizes a lot of their behavior and places unearned trust in their wisdom and loyalty. It is not unknown for people to make decisions committing corporate dollars or performance after little or no consultation with him. Either way, he has had to follow through on the commitment, much against his privately expressed wishes."

"How would you characterize him, then, as a chief executive?"

"I think it is important to say that his executive leadership is crippled by poor inquiry and avoiding conflict. Since no one knows what he actually wants, each acts independently, but this does promote strong autonomy among corporate executives. It is overdelegation, but still it has developed a strong management."

"Did he want to be president?" asked Walt.

"I don't think so, but I've never heard him say so directly."

"What's your best guess, then?"

"Well, it has been talked around and explained this way. He loved Randolph, the former president. There was nothing Randolph could ask of him that he was unprepared to do, and he appeared quite strong in that role, even able to carry out unpleasant assignments in behalf of Randolph. So perhaps the answer is that he became president because Randolph admired him. Stanley wanted to do whatever would please Randolph and Randolph may have seen his ability as a Number 2 and presumed he'd be the same way as a Number 1."

"I know this is a difficult question for anyone, but let me ask you to estimate his executive leadership. If you were to judge on a nine-point scale, from a great corporate leader to a failure, where would you place him?"

"You're right—it is a difficult question. I think I would place him somewhere below the middle—maybe a 3½ or a 4. He is not a visionary president who can actualize great possibilities. But by no means is he a failure, either, even though he is short on giving direction and helping people set higher goals. The constant encouragement and support he gives has led to an essentially autonomous corps of corporate executives who have done pretty well by the company. But it's also led to jealousies and empire building.

"There's something to be said for a free rein when it does not mean abandonment and when actions under delegation are encouraged and supported. Delegation in itself is a source of restraint. But even though subordinates have done sound things, they have been unable to exploit the potentials of the company because there has been no basis of central strategy, development, or overall leadership to strengthen the lateral potentials across subsidiaries.

"You can never measure the caliber of a chief executive unless you can see the strengths and weaknesses of the appointments he makes. When Stanley took office, most of the people either already had their assignments or had been designated as successors to those about to retire. It'll take another decade to verify my assumption, but I suspect he would not have chosen the same kind of strong people if he had been making the initial selection.

"As a matter of fact, I've heard a lot of complaining about organization structure. Fifteen years ago Randolph put in place the structure we now use. It hasn't changed since."

"What's the gripe?" asked Walt.

"Lack of integration. We need to be one company. For all practical purposes, we're several. The several would be stronger if headquarters successfully provided a basis of integration.

"Stanley realizes this. He made a move in that direction a couple of years ago vis-à-vis an executive VP. He encountered strong resistance. Subsidiary presidents felt their power threatened. None of them wanted any other one of them to be boss. Rather than solving the problem, Stanley backed off. Some think we have no future until the company makes a positive resolution."

"Will Stanley do it?"

"In my opinion, it's unlikely."

"How would you picture the impact of all this on the health of the corporation?"

"The answer probably will surprise you. I've seen many costly decisions that might have been avoided by a stronger and more directive chief executive. However, I've seen subordinates act with a good deal of initiative and wisdom. I can imagine they might not have been willing to exercise the degree of initiative had Stanley exercised unilateral control over them. This is a very hard question to answer, though, because many of the actual costs are not visible at this time. The question I have to answer for myself is, 'Have reduced cooperation and coordination produced significant costs?' There's too much empire building, too few rotations of personnel across subsidiaries, and occasionally the failure of two executives to go after something that together they could get but neither could land alone. Another question is whether the sacrifice of synergies has been worth the benefits the corporation has enjoyed by strong-willed executives who have essentially free rein. I don't think so, and that's why I put company performance in the middle or below. No one knows how to estimate these costs accurately or to translate them into lost profits. We're no longer in the fast lane but we're not moving backward either. That's about it.

"I've set up your conference with Lee Randolph for 2:30 Thursday. Is that okay?" asked Will.

"As you know, Lee, I have been conducting a review of corporate culture for the Board of Directors," said Walt. "It has been a very interesting project. People have been cooperative, and this has made it a most challenging project. I realize you have not been in the company for an extended period now, but you were in a critical role in deciding who your successor would be. He thought I might talk with you. May I ask as to the thinking that went into the selection of Stanley Mankoff?"

"I'm glad to be asked. It's a simple and straightforward story. Stanley had been a long-term corporate colleague and followed me in the various advancements that took me into the president's office. Whenever I moved, I arranged for him to come along. We were a good team."

"How would you characterize your teamwork?"

"First, Stanley was dependable. Whenever I requested he take an action, carry out a project, or help me, I knew he would do it in a good, sound, and timely manner, without friction, even when considerable delicacy was involved.

"He was loyal. I never considered he was leaking confidential information or speaking adversely about my leadership or the corporation. That kind of loyalty is indispensable from a senior executive.

"Third, he is a man of demonstrated competence. I would give him a general assignment and tell him that he had my 100 percent backing. I didn't have to spell out the details. Once he had the big picture, he was fully competent to execute with a minimum of assistance from me. I could free my mind of it and feel secure the job would be done in a professional manner.

"As I've noticed in many high-caliber executives over the years, Stanley had an uncanny knack for studying me and being able to anticipate what was important. He was also able to undertake whatever he brought to my attention. That may be why I rarely found it necessary to fill in the details. When I asked him to do something, he already knew what to do by having studied the concerns I expressed from time to time or the manner in which I thought about problems.

"At the time I felt him a thoroughly qualified executive for the presidency."

"Looking back, how would you react to his presidency?"

"I think he's done okay, but I can't say he has measured up to my aspirations for him. When he was my subordinate, he was decisive, firm, confident, and clearheaded. His presidential leadership has not been characterized by those qualities to the same degree. I have heard members of the Board confirm he is slow and sometimes reluctant to formulate and propose forward-looking actions. I am baffled by his pedestrian manner over the past several years in contrast to his surefootedness when working for me. I think he has been adequate, just not the best."

"What would you nominate as the corporation's most pressing problem today?"

"Organization structure stands out above the rest. There is widespread recognition it needs to be fixed."

"Had you discussed his possible candidacy with him before you recommended him?"

"Yes. It was a toss-up as to whether he would be the best person to fill my shoes or whether he would make a more significant contribution as the head of research and development. I think he wanted the latter, but something told me the former was the assignment for him. I can't reconstruct the details beyond this recollection. When I nominated him for the presidency, he was gracious and appreciative."

SUMMARY

The 1,9-oriented leader has a strong desire for acceptance and approval. This person is very sensitive to what others think. For these reasons he or she seeks to create an atmosphere of warmth, caring, and approval.

Motivations

Stanley's positive motivation was to gain acceptance and approval from others. The notion is that if people are treated nicely, organization productivity will take care of itself.

He feared and avoided disapproval and rejection. Feelings of rejection cause a 1,9-oriented person to be wounded and dejected.

Initiative

Stanley did little to exercise initiative directly. He asked others to take initiative and approved initiatives taken under delegation. His own lack of initiative, particularly with respect to strategy and planning, caused the company's subsidiaries to become disproportionately independent, to the detriment of the company. His initiative was limited to his job description, although he took initiative when asked to do so by those above him or when the consequences of not doing so were more severe. He took pains to mollify unpleasant news in order to avoid personal rejection.

The 1,9 initiative statement is: "I initiate actions that help and support others."

Inquiry

Stanley limited his reading to current events in national business periodicals. His natural alternative was to learn by talking and listening to others. He relied on others to research issues and provide briefings. He preferred these to be short and cryptic. He was a talker and a listener, not so much for gathering information as for social exchange.

The 1,9 statement is: "I look for facts, beliefs, and positions that suggest all is well. For the sake of harmony, I avoid challenging others."

Advocacy

While Stanley had convictions, he did not act on them. He became unsure and tentative when there was dissent. He would rather yield than to risk disagreement. On occasion this led to his being taken advantage of. The focus of his advocacy was on pleasing people. His enthusiasm for agreement sometimes led him to support positions before giving them careful consideration.

The 1,9 advocacy statement is: "I embrace opinions, attitudes, and ideas of others even though I have reservations."

Conflict Solving

Stanley abhorred conflict, so he went along with others even when he was right rather than to risk unpleasantness. He sometimes used third parties to assist in conflict resolution.

The 1,9 conflict-solving statement is: "I avoid generating conflict, but when it appears I try to soothe feelings to keep people together."

Decision Making

It was difficult for Stanley to make decisions because of his fear of possible negative reactions. Thus others frequently made costly decisions or commitments with which he disagreed. On potentially unpopular decisions he procrastinated. His failure to make a definitive decision on the corporate structure is an example of indecisiveness based on fear of being unpopular.

The 1,9 decision-making statement is: "I search for decisions that maintain good relations and encourage others to make decisions when possible."

Critique

Stanley's fear of rejection limited his critique and feedback to only positive encouragement. He bent over backwards to avoid being unpleasant to people, even those he personally disliked.

The 1,9 critique statement is: "I give encouragement and offer praise when something positive happens but avoid giving negative feedback."

Adverse Consequences

Stanley encouraged others to take independent initiatives that he should have had a hand in (p. 60).

Absence of deliberation between a boss and subordinates can result in initiatives that are less than fully sound because they do not represent the leader's thinking. Subordinates may not see what initiative is best to take.

When subordinates are taking independent initiatives based on their own perception of a situation, they are less likely to take advantage of coordinations that an executive can provide. Overlapping, redundant, or contradictory activities by subordinates may result. In the longer time perspective, these kinds of uncoordinated activities can lead to destructive competitiveness on the one hand or lessening of commitment and motivation on the other.

Stanley failed to provide direction to avoid costly corporate decisions (pp. 60–61).

When others take the freedom given them to make independent decisions, they may not see significant expense implications. This has the effect of costing the company needless expense if the leader is unwilling to overrule unwise commitments made by others. In Stanley's situation, he was caught between either permitting the continuation of a costly action or reneging on it and thereby reaping criticism or losing the warmth and approval of its originator. Caught in this dilemma, Stanley preferred to honor the commitment and thereby to retain at company expense others' good feelings toward him.

The point is that when a leader has a consultative role with subordinates, it is possible to influence decisions early and avoid either having to follow through at company expense or to lose the positive regard of subordinates.

> Rather than studying an issue deeply, Stanley preferred to have someone else investigate it and present him with a brief summary (p. 59).

Having a subordinate summarize a document or points of view on a proposal is common and often justified as a positive contribution to effective management of the executive's time. It can, however, leave much to be desired as the basis for strong executive leadership when it becomes a habit and a substitute for in-depth understanding. Those leaders who share Stanley's deficiencies of inquiry tend to miss the complexities and subtleties associated with a problem when they rely on subordinates' summaries and recommendations. Thus decisions reached are unlikely to be as sound as they otherwise might be. Equally, such an approach can lead to dilution of problem definition because subordinates are likely to propose no stronger solutions than they think their boss is prepared to implement.

> Stanley withheld or asked third parties to undertake essential but unpleasant actions in preference to being criticized for being mean, ugly, punishing, or destructive. ("If others do my dirty work, I'll smell like a rose") (p. 58).

A leader may avoid being labeled as harsh, arbitrary, negative, or unfeeling by shifting problems onto the shoulders of others who themselves may come to be known as "hatchet men." This means of getting results conveys to those on whom the negative impact is felt a sense of the leader's weakness or inability to face the deeper realities of organization life.

> Stanley had difficulty with personal time management (pp. 56–57).

Time management is widely regarded as a problem, and many approaches to solving it are mechanical in character, such as prioritizing problems. For example, the executive is advised to sort problems or decisions into three stacks and then to concentrate attention on those issues in the A (most important) stack first, on those in the less important B stack later, and on C stack items last.

Such mechanical procedures are by no means unimportant, but one of the main difficulties of such solutions is that too often they simply are not applied to work or, if they are, they are short-lived. Stanley is a good source of insight into why this occurs.

His underlying concern is to be liked by others and to avoid actions which might result in their dislike. We can presume that those items in the A stack are ones that are the easiest to deal with and that give him the most favorable attention. Those that might cause others to take offense Stanley would move into the B or C stack. Alternatively, he might leave them in the A-1 section of the A stack, with other tough items to be dealt with later.

By generalizing across other Grid styles, we can see other reasons for the all-too-often observed failure of mechanical solutions. A 1,1-oriented chief executive may avoid actions by overusing the C stack, where time takes care of some problems. A 9,1-oriented chief executive maintains control by increasing the size of the personal-attention A stack. This can result in a feeling that there is never enough time to do everything.

Overview of the 1,9 Grid Style

As with other Grid styles, the 1,9 orientation does not signify a specific type or personality. Different 1,9-oriented leaders may exhibit different characteristics due to background, interests, experiences, and a host of other factors, but these are nuances of the underlying assumptions.

Most 1,9-oriented executives promote friendship and camaraderie and, without intending to, have the effect of deemphasizing productivity. "You can't pressure people; if you do, they'll resist." This kind of supportive management unintentionally turns attention away from tasks in the interest of warm and friendly relations.

Many times these executives are fun to be with; they create a lot of spirit and project themselves as "decent human beings," considerate and thoughtful, doing the unexpected by way of gifts, remembrances, and personal touch.

A few 1,9-oriented leaders are gun-shy and seem overly apprehensive about rejection, which leaves them deeply wounded. These feelings convey the fact that the 1,9-oriented executive is tenderhearted.

SUGGESTIONS FOR CHANGE

A leader whose orientation is 1,9 might wish to consider the following suggestions for change.

Motivation

1. Being polite and solicitous may make you feel good, but others may see it as overdone. It may make them feel uneasy when it obscures issues that need solutions.
2. When a person acts according to high standards and expects the same of others, it is possible to achieve both acceptance and respect.

Initiative

1. You may see a possibility but discount it by saying, "I'd better not." Avoid stopping yourself before you start. Replace with "I'd better."
2. Take initiative in situations where you tend to back off. See if you do not receive increased respect.
3. You may be waiting for reassurance from others. Assess what to do on your own. Give yourself permission rather than seeking guidance from others.

Inquiry

1. Increase your preparation before meetings. This can help you feel more self-assured when you advocate your ideas.
2. Strengthen inquiry by asking questions that invite explanations. Others are ready to contribute what they know.

Advocacy

1. Rehearse your own convictions. Then express them.
2. Be among the first to speak when opinions are being presented. Don't wait to see what others have to say.
3. Let people know where you stand by saying, "I think. . . ."
4. Be as specific as possible: not "I think the B alternative is wrong (weak, limited)," but "The B alternative is a limited possibility because it omits the following. . . ."
5. If you tend to get wordy, cut to the heart of the issue when you speak.

Conflict

1. Accept that conflict is inevitable. Differences can be examined without creating tensions or risking rejection.
2. Smoothing over a difference doesn't solve it but does cause others to see you as weak.

3. If you find others disagreeing, restate your position and ask them for further explanation of their reservations.

Decisions

1. Speed up decision making by not postponing embarrassing or unpleasant decisions. The problems are likely to increase, and they might as well be dealt with now as later.
2. Don't consult others about decisions if they feel you are wasting their time or see no reason to be involved.

Critique

1. Feedback does not have to be painful. Describe your observations of others and the consequences of their actions.
2. Realize that feedback can be a two-way street. When problems arise, others may expect you to let them know how things look to you.
3. Others want to be helpful when you seek feedback from them. They will tell you as much as you want to know.
4. Point out barriers to good performance. Important difficulties are just as pertinent as positive aspects.

7
FATHER KNOWS BEST

"In all frankness, I'm surprised that Martin asked me to have this interview with you," said Lynn Murono, Martin Stein's inside consultant.

"I'm pleased he did. Why were you surprised?" asked Walt.

"Let me review Martin's ground rules for this discussion. He told me to feel free to discuss candidly with you my views in describing his leadership of this company. I asked him what this meant. He said, 'Withhold nothing.' That's what surprised me."

"It would help me to have a better idea of your relationship to Martin."

"My position is unusual," said Lynn. "I'm in but not in. Almost five years ago the company of which I was the CEO was brought in on a merger and set up as a subsidiary. They wanted me to continue, but I said, 'I'm not a person who can go from being a Number 1 to being a Number 2. I'd have to learn Martin's approach, but it's too late and I'm financially independent. If you want my knowledge and whatever guidance I might be able to offer for its success, I would be pleased to sign an employment contract for, say, five years.' We discussed this, and the terms of agreement were settled. I would provide consulting services and advice to the subsidiary chief executive and to Martin. This freed me to make recommendations with respect to both the subsidiary and the corporation. At the time it seemed an excellent idea. Martin has treated me with genuine consideration. I think I have offered assistance that has made a difference in a number of areas. The contract has two more months to run. I look forward to its ending, which will also put a QED on my active career in corporate life. I want the freedom to roam, since I can afford it."

"That's interesting, but I thought you were a member of the Board, too."

"Well, I forgot to mention that. Martin wanted me on the Board allegedly to strengthen it, but I now think it was to make the merged company a more attractive client to the financial houses. When it was decided to participate in your study, Martin concurred with the Board that I would be an ideal source of information. I've had five years of close observation without line responsibility. I think this was the reason. Although he concurred, I also know Martin was ambivalent about the Board's decision to participate in this project. He wanted to be in it for the stature it might add to his leadership image. But I think he worried that some of his limitations might also be documented. His internal battle between augmenting his stature and revealing his clay feet pushed him into participation, but the margin was small.

"That also provides a miniature sample of what I've seen many times. Battle after battle is waged in Martin's mind when he feels caught between a moral principle and a selfish gain. Sometimes the answer is on one side, sometimes the other. I'd say moral principle usually prevails."

"How do you judge Martin's success?"

"Good, but not great. The wise decisions have outweighed the unwise, but still there've been too few of the former. The net result is good, not great."

"Maybe that's the place to concentrate for a while. How does Martin go about making decisions?"

"That's a complex question to answer. Let me start by saying his decisions are basically good, because first of all he's a good finance man. He knows how to read the numbers. Furthermore, he loves them. If that were all there were to decision making, all his decisions would be excellent."

"Let me ask about the bad decisions. Some decisions that work out badly are inevitable because adverse consequences could not have been foreseen. Others go sour because the wrong decisions were made, even though the resources were available for making the right decision. When you say bad decisions, do you mean wise or unwise, or some of both?"

"You have to conclude some of both. His bad decisions tended to be in areas where subordinates and others disagreed with what he sought to accomplish or where they were unfamiliar with the territory. Either he never learned of their reservations, or he filtered them out. Martin tends to shut subordinates up who might disagree with him."

"Why is that?"

"Let me digress a bit. Martin places a premium on allegiance and loyalty. He goes out of his way to praise and commend those who comply with his wishes.

"Subordinates often misinterpret praise as appreciation of personal effort. The effect is to make subordinates weaker, not stronger, though I feel certain that he has no intention of doing that consciously and would deny it if accused."

"There are many activities we all carry out which are acts of compliance. What would be Martin's reaction to compliance?"

"Probably none," said Lynn. "When compliance is expected, its occurrence is treated as routine. It would be an insult or something close to it to praise compliance. That's how I see the difference between Martin's use of praise and what somebody else might do by way of expressing appreciation."

"How about reprimand? Is he a praise-and-reprimand person?"

"Yes, he is. If a person does something Martin doesn't think is correct or he fails to do something Martin wants, then he is quick to reprimand. I view his use of reprimand as bad. It's a slap on the wrist that says, 'Bad boy, don't do it again.'

"Another factor in his bad decisions is that he tends to keep subordinates apart who look at problems from different angles. I once heard a legal expert ask permission to get together with some financial people and come up with a package. His reaction was, 'Packages worry me. They tend toward the least common denominator. I'm asking you legal people to give me the best advice available. I want the numbers people to give me an assessment of worth, and personnel to give me their study of work force estimates of executive competence. Then I'll be in a position to reach conclusions on what actions to take.'

"That sounds like good, clean, responsible leadership. But looked at another way, this episode deprived Martin of the opportunity to hear the legal people, who in point of fact do have a lot of tax knowledge, argue with the financial people and to benefit from discussion.

"Too often Martin walks into problems that could be avoided if he brought people together to argue issues out. He sees no value in everyone being in on the know. As a matter of fact, I think he sees this as an unwanted risk; opposition might arise out of strength in numbers, and he might lose control.

"I guess you can see that Martin is the person in charge. He makes the ultimate decisions."

"Are you saying that he dominates his colleagues and associates?"

"My impression is that no one enters into give-and-take discussions with him. I think he feels conflict when things are said with which he disagrees, but he rarely expresses that disagreement in a direct manner."

"Then the interesting question is, how?"

"First, he determines the decisions to be made and actions to be taken. Then he is extremely generous in the sense of warmth, affection, and approval for others when they graciously accept what he wants. They are grateful and feel warm toward him. Their positive reaction indicates that they see him as wise and profound.

"I see the same thing in how he deals with the Board. As its designated leader, Martin is likely to give members a recommendation and ask for more or less rubber-stamp approval. He says, 'Trust me,' in effect, and on more than one occasion I've heard him say, 'I'm the only chief executive you have.' I think they have developed into a lip-service Board, and they more or less automatically give him approval based on faith, trust, and confidence. The more trust and confidence they extend to him, the less he feels compelled to reveal the rationale underlying his thinking. This has worked well enough because his good decisions outweigh his bad ones. As I said, he has earned the Board's allegiance and devotion for being so dedicated."

"How does he react to people who don't comply?"

"Usually, he puts the issue on the back burner. The subordinate who disagrees can reasonably rest assured it will not be brought up again. Either the subordinate will find himself with a narrower set of job-related activities, or he will quickly come to understand that his is not to question why but to accept and do."

"There are two other areas I would like to explore. One relates to delegation, the other to teamwork."

"Martin is a good delegator in the sense he has no reluctance to place responsibility in the hands of others and then give them free rein within limits of strict accountability. Once subordinates prove themselves by thinking the way he does and are trustworthy in carrying out what he wants them to do, they have become faithful followers. Under these circumstances he can delegate fully. He does so, saying, 'I have every confidence in you and I know you can do a good job.' Of course, they want to enjoy his continued approval. He doesn't ask subordinates to touch base with him when they come to a sticky point, but they do. It's my impression that he gains great gratification from providing subordinates the help they request, and I think they know that. It's an indication to Martin that his own wisdom and wise counsel are appreciated. He gives his unending loyalty to those who show this evidence of devotion.

"He's a great one for the mentor approach to developing managerial talent. He likes to have men fifteen to twenty years younger than himself in key posts. Without ever saying so, he conveys the notion his style of exercising leadership is worthy of emulation. He's learned to do it, and if younger people study how he does it, they, too, will learn how to do it. It's a complex and subtle process that goes on between him and them. The best I can describe it is to say it's a combination of subtle praise and reprimand, with a little bit of moralizing thrown in here and there.

"He tends to give great latitude to subsidiary heads when he can't keep himself closely informed. Yet the moment they get in trouble, he shortens the leash of his supervision through more frequent and detailed reporting."

"It sounds like an accordion approach to delegation. The amount increases when deputies do what he wants but reduces when they get in a jam. This way of delegating is true of leaders of many styles. What makes it unique to Martin?"

"It's the tendency to resume control in a problematic situation rather than to work with the deputy and find out what caused it. This doesn't mean he cuts the deputy out of the communication network. It only means he takes over the problem by telling the deputy what needs to be done; he then expects execution. As far as his dealings with the subordinate is concerned, the problem has become a closed issue. Martin just says, 'I think I'd better deal with it,' and from that point on the problem belongs to him. Many deputies have found this to be one of his ways of subtle reprimand, because he's not showing confidence or helping. In a silent way, as he takes over the problem, he is conveying the idea, 'You had your chance and blew it, so here's what I want to do now.'"

"What else about Martin's concept of teamwork?"

"He has meetings mainly to elicit information. Other meetings are for announcements about new projects, for putting something in motion, or making it official. The missing key is the matter of decisions or deliberation. He'll discuss for the purpose of inquiry but not deliberate about best approach. He shares top-level decisions with no one. I realize that this is not what is intended by the term *teamwork*, but it is his interpretation.

"Now I can say one or two other things about teamwork. His way of dealing with subordinates does induce rivalry, antagonisms, and jealousies. It's almost as though various subordinates are competing with one another for his favor. He deplores this, but I suspect he knows it's the pursuit of his approval that causes them to be antagonistic to one another.

I've heard him say, 'Now I want you two to park yourselves in a room, with no telephone calls, no coffee, no meals; and don't come out until you've agreed you're going to help one another.' "

"Has the corporation suffered from this lack of teamwork?"

"You never can really put a dollar on what might have been earned. At the very best it's a judgment call. I would say that it has been quite costly. The creativity of many people remains untapped, and who can say how the corporation might have developed had it been mined? I can't."

"Is there anything else to say about Martin's decision making?"

"I think he sees himself as someone who can groom young executives to become models of himself. At least this has been one of his major goals through his career, and I've known him over many years. I know he has helped the careers of many."

"Is this the image he projects?"

"To a certain extent, yes. Since you already know him, you realize he is a tall and wonderfully conditioned, handsome man. He stands 6 foot 3 inches, has white hair, and dresses in the most conservative and immaculate way. No one has seen him without his coat on since I don't know when. He has a sense of bearing. Being conspicuous, he enjoys being seen. Having the kind of ambition I have described, he enjoys being honored. Yet he would tarnish his image were he to blow his own horn. His reputation is enhanced by tribute coming to him almost like iron filings to a magnet."

"Let me shift the direction of the conversation a bit to examine conflict in more detail."

"His regime has not been characterized by anything approaching open conflict. Conflicts have all occurred outside his territory. He defuses conflict by withdrawing the issue. He doesn't relish having to argue his points. It's that simple. Over the years, those with whom he deals on a day in and day out basis tend to be people who acquiesce."

"Can you give me an example of some cherished project he wanted to undertake which others resisted?"

"I would say that on those rare occasions when he has become involved in a power struggle he has been unable to bear the thought of capitulating. His tendency has been to resist pressure, no matter what the expense in inner turmoil or even bottom-line dollars. He might defer the discussion for a while, but defer does not mean abandon, capitulate, or walk away. When he defers he is looking for some way of getting what he wants without creating a scene. I've heard him say, 'If I get opposition to this project, I'll destroy anyone who opposes me.' I think 'I'll destroy' reflects his inner conviction that it is better to remove opposition than to countenance or confront it. He doesn't really mean 'destroy' because it would tarnish his image. Perhaps his tactics provide a further basis for understanding why Martin rarely has anything approaching a dispute or encounter. He constantly wins by being able to achieve whatever he sets out to accomplish."

"But if he doesn't ask for advice and tends to be intolerant of opposition, how does he gain access to information that is critical for making complex decisions?"

"I would call him a super listener. He puts out a question in such a way that the other person usually has no earthly idea of what Martin is about. From the answerer's point of view, the question appears to be neutral. Then, as one question is answered, he asks others. It seems Martin's memory is a steel trap. He records all the answers in his head.

"Many questions may be remote from the central issue Martin intends eventually to explore. Some may be background and some may not appear important. He constantly probes, and the respondent really is hard put to know what Martin is after."

"Do people feel they're being quizzed?"

"No. He goes out of his way to ask questions of different people in various terms, approaching his basic interest now from the left side, then from the right side, sometimes from below, and sometimes from above. But it would be difficult for two people who had had an interview on the same topic to piece together where he was headed. The questions he poses are sharp, are well formulated, and can be responded to in factual terms. However, he avoids explaining the rationale of his queries to the person with whom he is talking."

"How do people react?"

"They love the opportunity to demonstrate the information they have at their disposal. To make that clear, I'd better give some examples of topics he deals with in this manner. In a recent meeting the topic was the long-term future of the microchip. Another topic was whether communication satellites represent a vulnerable aspect of contact between remote locations. You can see," Lynn continued, "that these discussions are not intended to reach a conclusion but to give him a feel for how others think about problems he believes to have pertinence. There's another angle, too. It gives him a way to test which subordinates think as he does. That's part of the cloning process.

"In other words, he is a solo thinker but not a solitary one. He does his own thinking; there's no question about that. He doesn't engage in the kind of give-and-take or parlaying of an idea that shapes and reshapes it as others make contributions."

"That's very useful. I take it from what has already been said that Martin is a man of great convictions. Do you see him that way?"

"No question. He does have deep convictions. I would say he also has prejudices or biases, even though he does his best to curb them."

"What convictions does he express?"

"He advocates hard work as an example to his subordinates. Few people leave the office before he does, and he is not inclined to depart before 6:30 or 7:00. Everyone knows the importance he attaches to hard work and long hours, and they busily engage themselves in doing the same. Of course, the place clears out pretty rapidly after he's gone.

"If there's one area of true advocacy, it's honoring the concept of the corporation. He extols its soundness, its growth, and its future so that others can say, 'We are as strong and as stable as an institution can be in this modern and fluctuating world.' I have also heard people say, 'I wonder if it was a wise decision to stay out of foreign markets when our competitors have demonstrated over the past fifteen years that global scale is a thing of the future.' But, of course, no one says this to Martin as he would listen but not react. People would feel embarrassed at having brought it up."

"Any other examples?"

"Oh, there are many. He advocates promotion from within. Employees are more than numbers; they are people who are investing their careers in the company. Therefore, promotion from within gives those who have been loyal an opportunity to develop themselves to the maximum.

"In spite of his plea for free enterprise, we are a birth-to-the-grave company. We have good medical benefits, dental benefits, retirement benefits. We have the concept of lifetime employment without importing it from Japan. We have matching educational grants by which organization members contribute to their university and the company adds encouragement by matching the contribution. Many feel we have the ultimate expression of corporate citizenship in concern for the individual. In a way, of course, this is true, but in another way it is not. If these kinds of activities were anchored to merit, that would be one thing. But that is not the case. These benefits are rights corporate members come to own after only five years of employment. In a moment of informality between Board members I heard that so much has been given away there is nothing more to give. I've also heard the remark that maybe that's not too much to pay—after all, it keeps us union-free. I dread to think of the depths of resentment if the company really fell on hard times or if an effort were made to retrench in any of these benefit areas. Such a possibility is by no means unrealistic when you consider the way competition has intensified its challenge to the corporation or the market share it has enjoyed. Do you realize there is speculation that market share has suffered a 15 percent erosion during Martin's decade?"

"No, I hadn't. Is this of concern to him?"

"I haven't heard him publicly express himself on this point, but if the 15 percent erosion is true, he is not spreading the bad news. I do know that he has no reluctance to commission the grand old consulting houses to carry out studies where his interests lie. He may ask for some advice in the marketing area. In due course, the consultants submit their findings. He tends to brace himself against their appraisals so as not to admit to himself he needs them. In the past, however, if they did not agree with the conclusions Martin had already reached, he was contemptuous, never of the consultants as persons but of their recommendations. It appeared to me that he would review the study's précis; if it didn't come out the way he wanted, that was the end of it. He would study no further. In that sense, he is a man of intense and often unjustified prejudices. But of course, he is gracious in thanking the consultant firm for the depth of their inquiry and breadth of their recommendations. He never opens up with those who disagree with him, and that results in my giving him counsel the way I do. As you can see, I'm really describing a very complicated man."

"Does Martin ever rely on feedback from others for steering his own activities? Does he provide others with feedback in order to provide them better direction?"

"The answer is quite clear. Feedback to him is out. Critique is out. This kind of give-and-take, particularly with regard to examining the effectiveness of actions which might look at his personal behavior is out of the question. I have discussed these concepts with Martin, and he sees them in a very negative light, as ways by which people attack one another as well as undermine confidence in him as a leader. Also, there are ways for people to compliment one another inappropriately and create soft and warm relationships that do not have the possibility of strong productivity outcomes. He does not engage in feedback, and I think he discourages others from doing so. Again, the formula fits: solo but not solitary."

"How would you describe your relationship with Martin? You said earlier that you had been with him for five years."

"He has sought my counsel at times. As a general instruction, not in regard to any specific issue, sometimes he says to me, 'When you think I am putting my foot into it, please say so. I'm suspicious of relying on the advice of those who might have hidden interests.' Many of the points I have made regarding his formality with others don't apply quite so well in characterizing our relationship. He has treated me as a confidant, and I have acted with great discretion in that relationship, since I'm neither fish nor fowl at this stage."

"Why is this so?" asked Walt.

"Because I'm not an employee in the conventional sense. I'm a person to whom he can either come or bypass, at will. If he does not come to me, it's of no consequence to either of us. I'm on a contract basis, but there've been extended periods when my advice has not been sought and other times when I have been contacted on a regular basis.

"I give him advice, but never directly, and I think he can answer questions I might have without any sense of feeling personally threatened. On a few occasions when I've offered him direct counsel, I have done so after reminding him of his ideals, his standing for what is right and true. This always stimulates his self-esteem and makes him more eager to have suggestions about what he should do. I do this only when I can foresee heavy cost to the corporation if he fails to reverse his prior position."

"Can you give me an example?"

"Usually I have been able to pose questions to him much as he poses neutral questions to others. They have the effect of aiding him to put things together. The questions I ask are not accusative, judgmental, critical, or negative, nor do they lead him to a conclusion that he may not wish to face. Nonetheless, I know that he has found this of value. I am perhaps the one person who has aided him this way, whereas most others would have been in his blind spot.

"He loves people but is remote from them. I think I have been able to provide a missing link in his effectiveness as a leader and executive. Now let me tell you the limitation in this. My questions for the most part have been with regard to personnel. I have avoided financial issues to which, however, I think I might have made important contributions. I have done so because when in some earlier setting I sought to offer this help, he let it be known that . . . well, he said, 'I have a banker helping me on that,' and then he moved back into interpersonal issues. Personally, I think I could have steered him away from some of his lemons, but let me leave it at that."

"Has he involved you in social affairs?"

"No. I think I mentioned that I have rarely attended a conference in the corporate offices. When we talk, we speak to one another here or in some outside location such as a local restaurant. On occasion we have met during vacations in Florida and Hawaii and once or twice in London."

"If I say the following, how do you react to it? 'I believe that Martin is a modern paternalist.' "

"I've not thought about him in those terms. But, no question about it: he loves his subordinates as children, wants loyalty from them, and wants to be loved by them. He does not want to accept direct help from them but is more than ready to give whatever he may be able to provide. He is a good 'father' in every sense of that as a managerial word."

SUMMARY

The basic assumption of a paternalist (or maternalist) is that he or she "owns" subordinates as if they are children to be looked after and cared for. In return for this care the subordinate is expected to be loyal and give respect. Martin emphasizes this in the family quality he has given the corporation: lifetime employment, unusual benefits, and so on, to reward loyalty.

Motivations

The positive motivation of a paternalist is to gain admiration and esteem through giving subordinates the benefits of one's experience, counsel, and guidance. When subordinates comply with what the paternalist expects, they are rewarded and are, in turn, expected to appreciate the help given them.

The leader seeks to avoid losing control, even if this demands transferring subordinates, narrowing their job descriptions, or even promoting them as means for reducing their influence. Substituting their own judgment in disregard of what they have been told demonstrates a degree of independence not acceptable to a paternalist.

Initiative

Martin exercises strong initiative with subordinates, to the point where he believes they can be relied upon to act as he would. Subordinates have a tendency to touch base with him on difficulties. This is due to his feelings of gratification at being asked to help and also because he tightens up his supervision if subordinates begin doing things in ways counter to his thinking.

The paternalistic approach to initiative is: "I stress loyalty and extend appreciation to those who support my initiatives."

Inquiry

Martin is a skilled questioner and listener, who questions in such a way that those being queried respond without knowing whether he approves. The purpose of questioning is not only to gain knowledge but also to test subordinates' thinking. He uses meetings for eliciting information but not for deliberation.

"The paternalistic approach to inquiry is: "I double-check what others tell me and compliment them when I am able to verify their positions."

Advocacy

Martin has convictions to the point of biases and prejudices. His advocacy of hard work conveys to subordinates that long hours are expected. As a way of reinforcing people's support of the corporation, he extols it for its strength. This kind of advocacy is almost overpowering, for it tells people that agreement is expected and counterviews not acceptable. Even with the Board he expects to be taken on faith, as shown by his comment, "Trust me."

The paternalistic approach to advocacy is: "I maintain strong convictions but permit others to express their ideas so that I can help them think more objectively."

Conflict Solving

Martin does not have to confront many internal conflicts. When conflict occurs, his strategy is to reduce or eliminate it. In one case where subordinates were in conflict he sent them to a room with instructions to remain until they had solved the problem, much as a parent might do with quarrelsome children. Other strategies for handling conflict are to withdraw the issue or terminate discussions leading to a win-or-lose conclusion. The withdrawal has almost a moralistic overtone, as though having to argue one's position when it is so obviously correct is demeaning. This approach has a stifling effect on those who have reservations and doubts, because to voice them is to express disloyalty.

The paternalistic approach to conflict solving is: "When conflict arises, I terminate it but thank people for expressing their views."

Decision Making

Martin is in charge and the ultimate decision maker. He determines what is to be done and how. Subordinates comply. He rewards them with approval. Those who have been delegated responsibility are free to make decisions but only under strict limits of accountability. Should they not perform these delegations in a satisfactory manner, Martin immediately shortens their leash by taking the assignment back under his immediate control.

Martin makes little use of discussion. He has a tendency to keep apart subordinates who look at problems from different points of view. For example, he prevents legal, financial, and personnel specialists from collaborating on the terms of merger. Because all fundamental information flows to Martin, everyone else's dependence vastly increases since no one has sufficient information to challenge his conclusions. Furthermore, with a fund of knowledge so much richer than anyone else's, he looks like an intellectual giant and is treated accordingly.

The paternalistic approach to decision making is: "I have the final say and make a sincere effort to see that my decisions are accepted."

Critique

Martin has a negative view of critique and feedback. The risk in critique and feedback arises when others confront Martin with weaknesses he wishes to deny. He fears to acknowledge them because doing so would cause an erosion of the loyalty and confidence a paternalist needs from those around him. On the other hand, his need for helpful support and insights to reduce bias and blindness is evident in his readiness to lean on a confidant in whom he could place complete trust and who therefore held no threat.

The paternalistic approach to critique is: "I give others feedback and expect them to accept it because it is for their own good."

Adverse Consequences

Martin engaged people in general discussions to learn how they thought about problems and to see if they thought as he did. His own thinking was not revealed (p. 77).

Many leaders favor like-minded subordinates. Once recognized, such people tend to learn to anticipate what the boss wants. This executive trait can bring forth a homogeneity of thought which can lead to unknown hazards. It is most risky when divergent positions are actively discouraged and varying points of view are forced out or underground. These circumstances frequently fail to probe potential dangers deeply, and thus eliminate true creativity.

When Martin couldn't be closely informed, he gave great latitude to subsidiary heads; but if they faltered, he immediately tightened supervision (pp. 74–75).

Some leaders use the rubber-band approach. They successively over-delegate and then overcentralize. This couples more leeway than subordinates are prepared to handle, on the one hand, with pulling back and reducing legitimate autonomy, on the other. The accordion effect makes it very difficult for subordinates under delegation to act with confidence. If they do so and falter, it appears there is more to lose than to gain, and therefore the attitude is likely to be "better not."

Martin advocated promotion from within, not so much because it afforded advancement to qualified people but because it provided rewards for loyal corporate members (p. 78).

Loyalty is admirable when it reflects dedication. Then loyalty means commitment. Some leaders confuse compliance with loyalty. For them compliance is important as an end in itself. This kind of loyalty has adverse consequences because it tends to be blind and may cause a person to fail to challenge short-sighted policies the leader believes sound. Under these circumstances, healthy dissent is equated with disloyalty. In addition, loyalty is no measure of competence.

> Martin told two subordinates in intense conflict to go
> to a room and not to leave until they had settled their
> problem (p. 76).

The nearly fatal weakness in this approach is the assumption that merely instructing subordinates to settle a matter is sufficient to get them to solve the problem and resolve any residual negative feelings toward each other. If they knew how to work the problem through directly, they undoubtedly would have done so long before.

The adverse consequences of abdicating rather than resolving conflict fall into two categories. By agreeing to back off and to avoid dealing with the issues that caused them to have difficulty with one another, subordinates may reduce the apparent friction but not solve the problem. Sitting down together may have the effect of intensifying the conflict rather than relieving it and turning people who merely had disliked one another into hated enemies.

> Martin instructed the legal and financial people to
> work separately in preparing a proposal, as he
> preferred to keep people apart and saw no value in
> everyone's being "in the know" (pp. 73–74).

A quite common leadership practice involves the chief executive dealing with each subordinate on a one-on-one basis only. An important deficiency in this practice is the fact that the leader fails to benefit from creativity that might take place as subordinates hammer away at solving a problem, each from his or her own specialized perspective. This benefit is minimal, of course, when the problem is relatively simple. The benefit grows almost geometrically as a problem becomes more complex and as the implications of one source of information become significant for another.

An executive development opportunity missed by the above approach is the broadening experience that can arise when specialists come at a problem from their own point of view but with the need to understand the perspectives represented by others. Few other methods can achieve such broadening as discussion of a complex issue on a one-to-all basis.

Overview of the Paternalistic Grid Style

The paternalistic orientation combines both 9,1 and 1,9 styles in an additive way. A paternalistic leader may take the appearance of a parental figure, benevolent autocrat, kindly despot, mentor, or teacher. "I own (or am responsible) for you and want to help your career (much as if you were a son or daughter). That's why I expect your loyalty as a matter of course." A family atmosphere may be a stressed corporate value.

Some paternalists strive diligently to gain admiration and emulation through giving the benefits of their experience, counsel, and guidance to chosen subordinates. There may be a tendency to preach and pronounce.

A statement such as the following is an indicator of paternalism: "My subordinates are reluctant to accept responsibility. They are bright and capable, with plenty of know-how, but they check with me first even when they don't need to. They won't take the ball and run." It is likely that subordinates want to please and feel the need to double-check because the executive may unwittingly undercut their confidence if they act autonomously.

SUGGESTIONS FOR CHANGE

The motivation of a paternalist is domination, mastery, and control exercised in a way that gains admiration. This means those with and through whom leadership has been exercised have become dependent on the boss. When they have done what has been wanted, they endear themselves to the paternalist, who may as a result become even more highly motivated to steer people. This kind of helping weakens their ability to exercise initiative and to contribute. Readiness to steer others is not likely to enable subordinates to develop autonomy and self-reliance.

The key problem to concentrate on to change toward a 9,9 orientation in values is becoming aware that others are remaining dependent. Stimulating more open participation earns the respect of subordinates and stimulates their development of problem-solving skills.

8

SAM LINDSAY—THE "ALL AMERICAN" EXECUTIVE

"How long have you been Sam Lindsay's VP of public relations?" Walt asked Pat Boyer.

"I've held that position for seven years here. He brought me with him when he joined this company. That's really a nontitle, though, because it doesn't tell much of what I do, or don't do. What it amounts to is that I am a right-hand man. My help is advisory in character, because Sam is his own man when it comes to public relations. Although his background is marketing, public relations is his forte. You might say that the way it's worked out, my job is kind of 'weaselly.' I rarely have to live with the consequences of my advice. He certainly doesn't have to make any commitments to me as to what he will or will not do."

"How did you come into this assignment?"

"I can give you a synopsis of a long story. I spent a few years as a journalist before joining our former corporate PR department to handle the annual report, speeches to shareholders, and other such writing. Because I had been involved in writing Sam's speeches for several years, he offered me this position when he moved and I've held it ever since.

"When it comes to seeing the motivations of people, Sam tends to be naive and gullible. Twelve years ago he almost suffered a career upset. He wasn't suspicious enough about the motivation behind advice given him, and he escaped from a corporate power play by the skin of his teeth. He realized that he tended to see the best in people and presume their good intentions. I'm suspicious. I smell the dirt. He finds this invaluable. He's frank to admit I have helped him avoid pitfalls he would have fallen into had it not been for my suspicious character."

"How would you say you get along?"

"Quite well. He wants to know what I think but doesn't want me to tell him what I think he should do. He's really a good listener, but if I come on too strong, he may turn and go in the opposite direction. That's about the size of it. I enjoy the fact that I don't have responsibility for consequences."

"Why was Sam brought in?"

"Seven years ago the principal owners decided they needed a more professional manager to lead the changeover from a privately held to a publicly owned corporation. The founder-chief owner had no heirs, so they decided it was important to go outside.

"Sam fit the bill for what they wanted. He had an excellent reputation and had had an outstanding career with one of the larger companies. He was known to members of our Board by his public service activities as well as through mutual Washington contacts.

"Beyond that, he had a number of desirable personal characteristics. He's a hard worker and well liked. He's handsome and has prematurely white hair and projects an image of strength, character, and maturity.

"There also was a natural match with his functional background. The company had achieved its strength through manufacturing prowess and product uniqueness and now was in an era of market and price competition. Sam's background in marketing was significant in his selection.

"Sam was a natural choice not only because of his experience and marketing expertise but because he was the right person to represent the company with investment bankers, in the senior management boards and conferences, and in Washington. He was also the right person for moving the company further in the international direction."

"How would you assess his impact so far?"

"The first impact he made," replied Pat, "was to set up an executive committee. This was his idea of participation and teamwork, away from the authoritarian tradition. The move was widely applauded."

"Does he continue to hold meetings?"

"Yes, even now, but to a lesser extent. I'm on that executive committee and I can say he enjoys the meetings. They're informal: no precise agenda, just the important nontechnical matters that members feel a need to discuss. He's pretty good on discussion procedure, too, although he tends to focus on noncontroversial topics. He doesn't intrude his own thinking into the discussion much. As far as decision making is concerned, he seems to search for consensus, or at least majority thinking, in order to exercise leadership. There's not a lot of conflict. His colleagues have learned that if they don't work out their differences in private, those differences will constantly arise as obstacles to effectiveness in these meetings. Sam is not one to force a final decision when his colleagues don't agree. That doesn't line up with his concept of executive suite democracy. I think the members are quite responsible in terms of either not bringing up disagreeable issues or getting together informally and coming to some basis of accommodation that permits them to cooperate.

"Let me back off from the word *consensus*. By it I don't mean decisions that have been hammered out to resolve reservations and doubts. Consensus is more like three-votes-to-two decision making. There's no actual voting, of course, but we are all more or less committed to testing the wind for what we have to say or withhold. Over the years something has become established that might be referred to as a floating consensus. For instance, if the issue is a manufacturing one, then those with background in manufacturing participate the most. If it's marketing, those who have had marketing experience talk it out. Experience determines the extent of participation."

"How does he do when it comes to delegation?" asked Walt.

"There I think you see the same thing in different clothing. He expects everyone to work within his job description, and in that sense he's a great one for delegation. He backs people with encouragement and camaraderie.

"Otherwise, I'd say he's a reactive delegator. He doesn't give assignments, except for special projects. But if someone begins doing something that needs to be done because no one else is doing it, he appreciates that. He doesn't see that either as sloppy management or as a desirability; he just accepts it. It is a kind of status quo thing. Once someone has started something, then it seems logical for him or her to continue it. It's the same whenever someone endorses an ideal or proposes an action. He'll say, 'That sounds like an important thing to do. Would you take it?' The other person says yes, and delegation has been accomplished.

"I want to point out that this is not deliberate delegation in the sense that Sam thinks through who the best person is for the assignment. He assumes a person making a proposal is interested in it, which is reason enough to endorse it. Another side to the coin is that he won't be embarrassed or criticized if he asks the person who made the recommendation to take the next step."

"How does he think about organization generally?"

"He's been back and forth on that. As I've said, he likes meetings; he enjoys discussions; he believes in an open-door policy. On the other hand, this open-door practice has played havoc with his time management. The lights never go out; Sam has excessively long hours; he can't say, 'No, I can't see you,' to anybody. This produces more and more time pressure and gives him less time to think. Since everyone seems to want more time of those who are at the pinnacle than of others, the open door just hasn't worked for him.

"He finally had to move away from open-door informality and get the chief-of-staff notion built into Al Hall's job of executive VP. Al's the funnel through whom big issues are placed in priority and brought to Sam's attention. This practice has also resulted in a diminished role for the executive committee, though Al often does run issues by members to get their reactions."

"Is he overreliant on the executive VP?"

"Yes," said Pat. "He wants alternatives, and the manner in which these alternatives are framed often tips the balance.

"But I haven't told you about his decision-making guidelines yet, have I? This is another way in which he seeks to protect himself. This is a checklist he brought home from a short course on 'How to Conduct Meetings.' It helps him feel secure that he's not getting entrapped. Would you like to hear them?"

"Yes. I'd be very interested in knowing what they are."

"Here goes: (1) If at all possible, use a prepared agenda as the basis for a meeting. (2) Stay on the topic under discussion and be alert to red herrings. (3) Be alert to hidden agendas and vested interests. (4) Encourage dissent without allowing a few people to dominate the 'air time.' (5) Keep discussion open until everyone has a chance to speak. (6) Listen to others before expressing yourself. (7) Get a second opinion before reaching a conclusion on a recommendation. (8) Don't rely too heavily on any one person. (9) Work toward getting all members 'on board.' " Pat paused for a moment.

"That's a pretty long list," said Walt.

"But let me give you the last one. Number 10 is, 'Sleep on it to avoid a knee-jerk reaction.' "

"Is he able to keep these in mind and be guided by them?"

"No. He has them printed on a card set in a Plexiglas paperweight on his desk. It is a reminder to be more careful. When his people are talking about a session, they get to the point where they'll laugh and say. 'We made it through the first eight, but flunked Number 9.' "

"What other practices has Sam brought in that have made a difference?"

"A key one is his dedication to the use of a budget as a basis for orderly business practices of planning, forecasting, and control. This has made the Board happy, I know. Prior to Sam's tenure an effort was made at budgeting, but by the end of the year there were always a number of surprises that broke the budget. The situation bordered on chaos. If it weren't for the fact that no dishonesty was involved, you'd think people were out to manipulate the budget.

"Sam put an end to that. He insists on a budget protection process begun six months in advance of the next year and reviewed three months in advance; he himself works through the final details. He frequently makes changes, in consultation with the appropriate people, so that by the time the budget is submitted, the Board can place confidence in it as a solid plan. There is likely to be little departure from it, particularly on the expense side. Sam allows a little item substitution to give the divisions some flexibility, but the expense limits are treated as absolute ceilings."

"Let's look at another facet. Does he speak out on issues? Does he inspire others? Is he imaginative?"

"None of the above, or at least no to most of your questions. He's a member of the conservative school when it comes to economic theories. He agrees with many others of his stature that market mechanisms are superior to deliberate national planning or national economic policy."

"How does he feel about Japan? Japanese economic planning seems to use umbrella-type strategic thinking provided by the Ministry of Industry and Trade."

"He's baffled by explanations that relate it to oriental culture, but as far as mechanics are concerned, I think he feels that Japan was so far behind that it was natural for them to catch up. Now that they are at a competitive level with the developed world, he feels that there is likely to be a faltering in the next few years and that the planning of the Japanese government will begin to have a constraining effect.

"I don't mean to give the impression that Sam is a thinker who has made a deep analysis and assessment. That's not the case. He takes his beliefs from his associates—directors, chairmen, presidents—in other companies and from highly placed persons in government. His formulations reflect values he shares with the business community. Convictions learned from them allow him to have convictions and speak them freely, and without contentiousness, for that matter.

"Let me give you an illustration of where he gets his topics. He doesn't understand how they got it, but he truly admires the Japanese emphasis on quality. So he picked up the quality pitch. Three years ago he launched a 'Quality First and Foremost' program. This was going to be our competitive advantage. He created a special task force to engineer the entire effort. The program was launched at a banquet of the upper echelons of the company, 700 in attendance. He addressed the group, said he stood strong and firm behind the quality program and wanted everyone to do likewise. The company organ rehashed quality time and again. QFF buttons were awarded to anyone who took the pledge for 'Quality First and Foremost.' People talked quality. We got into quality circles for a while, but like so many other campaigns over the years, this scheme faded away about 18 months ago."

"Okay, let's move on. What about his approach to managing conflict?"

"Very troubling to him. As I mentioned, in his executive committee meetings he tries to avoid issues that might cause members to get into win-or-lose scraps. Yet over the years there have been a number of classic conflicts between subordinates. It seems to me he hasn't dealt with any of them in a good manner."

"Describe a couple of those."

"The first one involved Al and me. Al has had and continues to have a close relationship with Sam. He saw me as a threat because of my direct pipeline to Sam. Al would say, 'There can only be one executive vice president, Sam.'

"This riled me because I didn't have any particular love for Al. He seemed to me to be an opportunist who always wanted to have a one-to-one relationship with whomever he was dealing. Sometimes that proved difficult. Sam coaxed us to get along, but we didn't. Finally, he got us together and said, 'Look, I want you guys to get together, and I want you to work out how you're going to do it.' He presumed that delegating this problem would resolve the disagreement. Usually it doesn't, but in this case it did.

"I made it clear to Al that my job was strictly a staff assignment and that Sam wanted my assistance and support as a person who could put his thinking into prose. I also made it clear I had no real interest in line matters or getting involved in operational problems. I was able to satisfy Al that there doesn't have to be conflict between the two of us. Bottom-line thinking, worrying, and sweating is for him, not for me. When we talked over why I have to have a one-to-one relationship with Sam, to satisfy the requirements of speech writing and public relations, my role became so obvious he could put no other interpretation on it.

"As a result, I think Al has come to realize that my contribution really is helpful to Sam, that I keep Sam from making statements that might be embarrassing or that would draw criticism. This isn't exactly Al's forte, either, because he tends to think more in terms of 'what's in it for me?' He now feels I contribute something that he is not able to provide.

"In other words, I solved a conflict that Sam handed over when he seemed unable to face up to it."

"You said there were two or three of these. Could we explore another one?"

"Yes. I wasn't able to help with these others, because any participation on my part would have been a violation of my job description. One of them involved two vice presidents who were competing over turf—jurisdiction, responsibility, reporting arrangements, empire, and so on—before Al became executive VP. What Sam did was to arrange a job offer for one of the VPs from one of his business associates in another company. Having that in his pocket, he 'invited' the VP to resign. However, he obscured his motivation for handling it in this way by putting it in these terms: 'An associate of mine in another company needs a person with your talents, and I told him that I thought you would be interested. While it would be a sacrifice on our part, I would be prepared for him to offer a job to you.' This man, Sheldon by name, said, 'Sam, you're firing me. I don't want a job elsewhere.' This was very disturbing to Sam, who tried to maintain the charade. Sheldon left but refused to take the assignment Sam had worked out. He is now the head of a company and doing very well.

"The situation wasn't handled well. The company lost an invaluable talent when Sheldon left. Sam tried to split the two competing VPs up rather than to confront the issue openly and get to the bottom of it. If he could have gotten those two guys to examine their relationship and why they were constantly going at one another and what each would have to do to support the other, Sam might now have greater depth in the succession area. To confront them openly would probably have been too tension-inducing for him to tolerate. He seeks easy, personal relationships, and he doesn't like tension. Furthermore, I think he developed the job-option tactic because he never likes to define anything too sharply. That may be another aspect of his approach to conflict, because if he defines something sharply, others can disagree with it and he's into conflict again. Rather, he likes to keep things loose, a little tentative and gray."

"Given that view of him, Pat, how would you describe his exercise of initiative? Does he go after problems or let them come to him?"

"The answer to that is neither," said Pat. "He reacts when one appears. On the other hand, he doesn't just sit and wait for problems. What he likes to do is touch base with those who report to him. When everything is okay, that's fine by him."

"Let me work on another angle of this. Is he moody? Does he have ups and downs? Is he even-keeled?"

"He's pretty unflappable. He rarely bites at anybody, nor does he seem to be depressed or morose. He has a calm, even-tempered approach with a little humor on a day-by-day basis. He doesn't work at a killing pace, but then you never think of him as being particularly idle. There's a comfortable tempo about the way he conducts corporation affairs. He doesn't want to solve problems yesterday, nor does he want to see them postponed until next year. He feels secure by learning what they are and then chewing on problems until an acceptable approach for dealing with them has been agreed on. I want to emphasize that the other person is basically the source of initiative for identifying the problem that Sam should give attention to."

"How does he go about learning?"

"He's not an intellectual heavyweight, and he proudly justifies disinterest by emphasizing, 'I'm a practical man; I'm an empirical man; I live in the world of bottom-line realities.' He doesn't dig into history or economics. He's had an awful time trying to decide about expanding the business into Asia. I would say he's not informed deeply enough.

"I think he's a good listener, but his way of talking with people creates a little distance, a remoteness."

"What about feedback and critique? Does he ever receive any?"

"No, and I'll tell you why. You get a feeling that people are polite and want to tell him what he wants to hear rather than what he may need to know. Not that they can't be open with him, but they're not open to the extent that he learns the bitter truth when it may be evident to them. What it boils down to is that what he does learn may not be all that significant."

"I forgot to ask; how old is Sam?"

"He is fifty-seven. He has eight more good years until retirement."

"I think I comprehend Sam's management style save for two angles. What really makes him tick, and what ticks him off?"

"I told you that twelve years ago he got caught up in a corporate power play, but it was not of his own doing. It was embarrassing to him that he didn't anticipate the situation, and he took a lot of criticism for getting sucked in. I think embarrassment and criticism are two things that he simply is uncomfortable with. That's one side of it. The other side is he wants to be popular, to be applauded for being basically a nice guy—you know, open door, speeches, friendly with everybody, that sort of thing. Now you can see why I provide the kind of support for him that I do. I anticipate potentially embarrassing or sensitive problems that he is unlikely to recognize. On the other hand, I don't share credit for actions he takes. If they are sound, the credit goes to him."

"Is Sam respected?"

"Best answer would be, admired, yes; respected, not really. He's admired for what he stands for and the fact that the company has moved along smoothly since he came on board. There have been no work stoppages. He's admired for his position in the business world and in our community. He isn't respected as a dramatic or dynamic leader who arouses people to energetically pursue his visions of what the company could become."

"How would you characterize Sam's presidency to date?"

"The health of the corporation from a profitability angle is average and maybe a bit above. I think the budget has been his albatross. He is conservative-minded and hasn't wanted to let expenses grow or money be allocated to new areas or projects that in his mind are unproven or risky. We haven't been able to deepen market penetration through better product design and engineering or improved quality. For the same reason we haven't been able to enter new market areas. What looks like conservative business practice, when conventionally viewed, has had a stifling effect on the company when seen from a different angle.

"We've dropped in rank in the *Fortune* 1000 but we've progressed in dollar volume even taking inflation into account. Union relations I think have gone down. There've been a number of tough confrontations recently. When issues have become sharply posed, and the union has taken a put-up-or-shut-up posture, we've always bent enough to get a resolution. I think we have progressively lost some of our contract-based freedom to exercise strong initiative in running this company. It's just an observation, though."

"If you were projecting," Walt asked, "what would you see in Sam's future?"

"I expect things to go along much as they have—safe decisions arrived at without great conflicts. I think we'll continue to see the company operate with moderate success. I worry about the union's becoming more militant, but that may be a needless concern. The best I can say is that Sam has been a good, average leader up to now, and I suspect he will continue to be so through his tenure."

"Do you plan to stay on, Pat?"

"Yes, I hope to. I enjoy this assignment. As Sam's career progresses, I suspect that I may be called upon for support, since I know his mind possibly better than he does. . . . What I mean is, since I can organize the contents of his mind in a manner different from the way he organizes it, I think I make an important contribution. Furthermore, he is able to use me as a sounding board. Finally, I can see him moving toward some traps and pitfalls. With my early warning devices, I can alert him to risks that remain hidden related to his own weaknesses. Furthermore, I've seen enough of the business world that there no longer is any thought in my mind that I want to get more personally involved in the dog-eat-dog competition. I'm not that kind of person, and I don't want to be enmeshed in that way."

SUMMARY

The conformity pressures felt by a 5,5 leader like Sam ensure that progress under his or her leadership will be slower than under more dynamic leadership. Sam lets others set the tone and tempo in preference to exerting influences that can exploit new developments or change old ways of doing things to bring them in line with current possibilities. When the leader's actions do not model excellence, the almost inevitable result is that the organization settles, if not into mediocrity, then certainly at a level below its potential.

Motivations

Sam's positive motivation is wanting to be popular, to be in step, and to be seen as doing the right thing or taking the right action, as defined by immediate colleagues, the broader constituency of the corporation, and the community at large.

His negative motivation is to avoid criticism or embarrassment. To be embarrassed or criticized implies that one is not in synchrony with the prevailing views of others.

Initiative

Sam's approach is to maintain a comfortable tempo in his work pace. His initiative is reactive rather than proactive. This differs from a pure stimulus-response approach, for the 5,5-oriented leader does work to prevent circumstances from reaching crisis proportions before taking action. However, the demonstrated initiative seldom originates from the leader but from other people or outside forces. When initiative is exercised, it is cautious.

In delegating tasks, Sam is appreciative and supportive when someone sees something that needs to be done and proceeds to do it. He is reluctant to seek problem areas but responds when they come to his attention. He is not known for emotional highs and lows but maintains an even temperament. Another example of his reactive initiative was the "Quality First and Foremost" program. When the Japanese emphasis on quality became highly visible, he latched on to the idea but in a prosaic manner and without follow-through.

The 5,5 approach to initiative is: "I seek to maintain a steady pace."

Inquiry

Sam's use of inquiry is superficial, with beliefs drawn from others he deems important rather than from personal investigation of issues. By touching base with others, he is able to stay reasonably informed. He does not probe questions in depth but simply accepts the views of colleagues in other companies and highly placed persons in government. The superficiality is also reflected in his lack of deep understanding of economics and history. The disclaimer of being a "practical" man allows him to ignore deeper issues of leadership.

The 5,5 approach to inquiry is: "I take things more or less at face value and check facts, beliefs, and positions when obvious discrepancies appear."

Advocacy

Positions Sam advocates are consonant with the convictions of esteemed persons in whose ideas he places credence. Sam is able to support reliable, established points of view but avoids responsibility for them should they be challenged. Some of his decision-making guidelines show that Sam expresses his own convictions in tentative ways. Among the guidelines relating to advocacy are "Listen to what others have to say before expressing your own conclusions" and "Always get a second opinion." Sam does not intrude his own thinking much into the discussions in meetings, particularly at the beginning. Exemplifying a 5,5 approach of testing the water, he prefers to ease in rather than to take the plunge.

The 5,5 approach to advocacy is: "I express opinions, attitudes, and ideas in a tentative way and try to meet others halfway."

Conflict Solving

Sam's basic values in dealing with conflict are accommodation and reasonableness. Rather than confronting two antagonistic subordinates, he delegated responsibility to them to resolve their conflict. On another occasion, rather than confronting the issue squarely, he arranged for one of two conflicting parties to be offered a job in another company. By neither taking sides nor opting for extreme positions, the 5,5 leader expects to be perceived as fair and reasonable. This inhibits others, who are reluctant to be viewed as contentious.

The 5,5 approach to conflict solving is: "When conflict arises, I try to find a reasonable position that others find suitable."

Decision Making

Safe decision making characterizes Sam's approach. Decisions are discussed frequently on an informal one-to-one basis but not deeply deliberated in order to increase the likelihood of their being truly sound. He seeks the acceptable course of action based on majority thinking. Sam avoids forcing decisions upon others and prefers to find positions that earn ready endorsement to get everybody "on board." The floating consensus method used by Sam and his staff, which involves the experts' contribution to the problem, is an example of a splitting mechanism to gain acceptability of decisions. The fact that he relied upon the decision-making guidelines is an indication of a mechanical rather than dynamic process of decision making.

The 5,5 approach to decision making is: "I search for workable decisions that others accept."

Critique

Sam touches base with subordinates to determine if things are going well and, if so, he is supportive. Because of his approach people tend to tell him what he wants to hear rather than what he needs to know. As illustrated in the situation between Pat and Al, feedback is informal or indirect. Sam acknowledged their problem and his unhappiness with it, but, having raised the issue, he asked them to solve it themselves. This way of avoiding entanglement in the problem makes it unnecessary for him to become emotionally involved.

The 5,5 approach to critique is: "I give informal or indirect feedback regarding suggestions for improvement."

Adverse Consequences

Although issues were deliberated among several subordinates, Sam relied on a topical specialist to have the final recommendation in decision making (p. 89).

There is little doubt that a person who deliberates a problem from a specialist point of view is likely to know more about that problem than someone with a different background. In recognition of territory, expertise, experience, or commitment, a leader or group may defer to a person who is especially concerned with an issue. At top levels, therefore, marketing people hold more sway in discussions of marketing issues, manufacturing people in discussions of manufacturing issues, and so on. This may lead to the untested assumption that the expert knows best when it comes to reaching the final conclusion. Often this is a valid generalization, but on other occasions a myopic specialty perspective prevents the perception of a problem's connections and interdependencies with other specialties. Another risk in excessive reliance on the expert is that experts themselves are likely to have their own stereotypes and prejudices that color their judgment but that are off limits for others to challenge.

When a chief executive or top team members operate according to a turf-based concept of decisions, the richness of deliberations that might produce sounder decisions is likely to be sacrificed.

> When a subordinate took initiative for something that needed to be done, Sam viewed it as good delegation to give that person responsibility for completing the action (pp. 89–90).

The question should always be asked, "What is the best way to bring a proposal into action?" The proposer may be the best executor, but it also may become clear that other persons are far better executors than the proposer. The proposer may not have the time, interest, or background to carry through on the execution, even though the problem itself may merit action. Also, if such mechanical connections between proposer and executor become the rule, people may hesitate to initiate on the premise that whenever they do so, they are automatically commissioned to carry out the action or solve the problem.

> Sam relied on his executive vice president to bring issues to his attention, with alternatives for action ranked in advance according to priority (p. 90).

Many chief executives rely on a chief-of-staff concept of organization as an efficient way of bringing order to issues that need their attention. The advantage is that the chief executive's time is freed from developing background considerations by which priorities are established. Therefore more time is available for dealing with these issues as well as others, and for external obligations and opportunities.

One limitation is that the chief of staff's priorities may differ from the chief executive's likely priorities had he or she studied the same problems. An overdependency on the executive vice president may lead subordinates to the justified conclusion that the chief executive has essentially abdicated.

Another limitation is that the chief of staff, having studied what and how the chief executive thinks, may delete from consideration or postpone new problems that do not fit a previously established order of priority or pattern of thinking.

Even when the chief of staff puts forward alternative ways of dealing with problems, there is another potentially adverse consequence: the chief executive may not have developed sufficient intimacy with the problems to be able to weigh the alternatives.

> Among Sam's several decision-making guidelines there were some which steered him away from openness and anything resembling a confidant relationship (p. 90).

One indication of the adverse consequence of poor teamwork is the need for a confidant. The leader's overdependence on the confidant may put the latter in a controlling position rather than in the role of a useful sounding board.

Another disadvantage is that to be effective the confidant must be totally selfless and unambitious for his or her own career. Confidants have been known to hide their ambitions and apparent selflessness only to take advantage of their special relationship with the chief executive when it serves their own benefits. Sam's desire to avoid a confidant relationship was motivated by the fact that he had previously suffered embarrassment because of misplaced trust. The purpose of his guidelines was to help him avoid repeating the mistake.

When top-level relationships are open, candid, and unsecretive—attributes that characterize an effective team—then there in fact is no need for the confidant role. With team collaboration no one desires to or is in a position to take unfair advantage of what he or she knows in comparison with what others don't.

Many of Sam's other guidelines serve the same purpose as the confidant guideline. They are more or less good commonsense notions that can lead to positive results and sound behavior when the process dynamics are understood. Taken literally, however, they are likely to lead to mechanical behavior which can yield poor as well as good results more or less on a fate premise.

> Sam adopted the "Quality First and Foremost"
> program without in-depth understanding of what
> was involved or the need to see it through
> (pp. 91–92).

Without deep understanding of what is essential for achieving high quality in a consistent way, Sam misinterpreted quality as something that may be "promoted" into being rather than earned. This kind of public relations approach to quality gets attention, but rarely leads to commitment.

Quality in this instance is a more or less virtuous aspect of corporate well-being which, like many other concepts of business logic such as "management by objectives," "zero defect," zero-based budgeting, high inventory turnover, management information systems (MIS), and decentralized structure, is only the tip of the iceberg. At least two considerations are often neglected when a business concept like one of these comes under the spotlight. One is that, for emphasis (or centralized structure), the notion is isolated from the context of the many complex variables that need to be considered simultaneously. The other is the assumption that emphasis and prescription by top-level executives will motivate change. The quick-fix approach leads to a series of eighteen-month fads while fundamental problems tend to remain.

> When two subordinates were feuding over turf, Sam
> made it possible for one of them to be offered a job in
> another company as a means of solving the problem
> (p. 93).

Turf conflicts go with territory, of course, and exist in almost any company and at all levels. An effort to solve such boundary disputes by eliminating one of the protagonists does have the effect of removing the problem for the time being, but it also has the adverse consequences of sacrificing potentially worthy people in the interests of ending disputes. The premise of this tactic is that people are basically selfish and no amount of looking at the real issue of how best to deal with territory problems is likely to yield a solution. This viewpoint only ensures a significantly adverse consequence, i.e., the biggest and strongest fighter will win, and the reasonable problem analyzer is likely to get the transfer.

Overview of the 5,5 Grid Style

The 5,5-oriented leader is likely to be a reflection of the environment or circumstances in which he or she operates rather than an influencing force. Depending upon what is thought to be acceptable to colleagues and in accord with the norms of the organization, 5,5-oriented leaders may exhibit a broad variety in their appearance, demeanor, and interests.

Maintaining one's reputation and prestige within the system is important to stay in good standing. To be affable and companionable, the 5,5-oriented executive strives to become an interesting conversationalist in order to make many friends. Thus, he or she might be described as a sociable, outgoing mixer and glad-hander.

The executive assumes that others are realistic, expecting to exert some effort. However, he or she also assumes that extreme positions promote risk and are to be avoided, even if it means making modest progress and staying within traditional grooves and ruts. The precedents and practices of the organization are embraced in an uncritical manner because "that's the corporate way" or "that's how things are done around here." Moreover, when the executive is acting within the boundaries of the status quo, he or she can exude confidence and strength.

The guiding rule is caution. The leader avoids taking a chance, being separated from the mainstream, or becoming a target of ridicule. Being out of step, sticking one's neck out, or being on the limb that is sawed off can place one's status in jeopardy. Tentativeness and uncertainty characterize a 5,5-oriented executive, for whom change can create anxiety and lead to vacillation and inconsistency rather than surefootedness.

SUGGESTIONS FOR CHANGE

The 5,5-oriented leader who wishes to reach beyond a pattern of accommodation to the status quo and seek a more dynamic approach to leading may wish to consider the following.

Motivation

1. Consider whether the reactions from others communicate respect or simply reflect acceptance of your conformity-based actions. Earning respect involves voicing one's genuine convictions rather than what one thinks others want to believe.

Initiative

1. When something needs to be done, act on the logic of the situation without overreliance on traditions, precedents, and past practices.
2. Others respect you for taking a problem in hand rather than waiting for someone else to bring it to your attention.

Inquiry

1. Be more thorough to avoid being insufficiently informed. When you think you have learned something, ask additional questions to be sure your understanding is complete and you have the essential details.
2. When you write something, ask yourself if it was written to make it attractive or palatable. If so, what were you really trying to accomplish? See if others interpret what you've written the same way you do.

Advocacy

1. Express convictions, on the premise that others are interested in knowing what you really think. You may gain in spontaneity by saying what you really think rather than editing or shaping convictions to make them agreeable.

Conflict

1. Disagreement can lead to valuable innovation. It is possible to disagree with someone and then explore the background and rationale of a disagreement in an open and candid way without being hostile.
2. What produces hostility is the implied ". . . and you are wrong." What reduces it is to ask about the background of a conclusion or about a

person's reservations and doubts regarding his or her own position. Provide the same without having to be asked.

3. It is possible to evaluate any position without regard for who will gain points, or lose face. Openness and candor remove win-or-lose attitudes from serious discussion.

Decisions

1. Although you may ask for input, there are some decisions that only you can make. For these it is inappropriate to ask others to share beyond input.

2. You gain respect by making decisions when others expect you to make them, without delays.

3. When you make your decision known, the understanding of others is likely to increase if you provide your reasoning. It's a good idea to let others know the alternatives you examined and the reasons for their rejection.

4. You can revise your decision to everyone's benefit if people disagree with it and can find flaws in your reasoning.

5. Reexamine how much and to whom you delegate authority. Equity and equal burden are not to be disregarded, but the soundest criterion for delegation is the greatest degree of resourcefulness.

6. Teamwork based on majority thinking may be in the right direction, because two heads may be better than one. However, two heads may be worse than one if teamwork is based on compromise. Consider concentrating more attention on the reasons some advocate a certain policy and on the misgivings of those who disagree. You may learn much by exploring the bases of their skepticism.

7. Majority-based decision making can be harmful when to "go along in order to get along" is the basis of agreement. Decision making improves when people can express themselves openly and candidly in the search for the most valid solution to a problem. A strong leader works to shift the basis of decision making from the former to the latter.

8. It is important to dig out reservations in order to reach an unqualified consensus. When a member enters into team-wide consensus, he or she accepts responsibility for consequences. This means the member has a good understanding, without having to be told, of what to do, how to do it, and with whom.

Critique

1. Feedback gives you an opportunity to express your reactions to the thinking of others and, conversely, it provides insights into how they

react to your thinking. It allows you to check what you plan to do before taking action and reduces or eliminates needless mistakes.

2. One way to get sound feedback is to ask for it, and then to listen to what is offered. Critique is particularly valuable when it is negative and raises doubts. Rather than accepting it publicly but privately rejecting it or ignoring it, ask yourself, "Is this the sound interpretation, or am I kidding myself?"

3. When you show people you want feedback and critique, it is likely to alter the character of your teamwork, since members will want to solve the real issues that hamper productivity.

9

DON'T DO SOMETHING, JUST STAND THERE

"When Frank resigned, it caught everyone by surprise. No one was aware of his intention to get out. That's why it produced a shock effect," said Harry Hamblin, Frank Collins' successor. "I must say that the company doesn't look the same to me as it did a month ago."

"Are there problems you've had to face on an emergency basis?"

"Yes, a number of needed decisions had piled up, and I've had to sort them out. I'm pretty much through them now. In the process, I've gotten to know even more about Frank."

"Well, it's Frank that I'd like to concentrate on in this discussion."

"How can I help?"

"I would like to know how Frank exercised leadership—first the mechanical details. Then I'd like to explore the more dynamic aspects," said Walt.

"The place to begin is where Frank took over, seven years ago. The person he succeeded died unexpectedly of a heart attack on a tour of corporate operations. Frank, as Executive Vice President, was automatically made President. There had been a history of such successions. We're an old company in the materials handling business, and an established pattern tends to perpetuate itself.

"During Frank's tenure we have had prosperous times. From a financial point of view, the company looked better the day he left than the day he took over."

"That's an interesting scenario: seven years of tenure, seven years of prosperity, and an unexpected resignation."

"There's more to it than meets the eye. Based on what I know now, Frank had a relatively clear perception of the dilemmas of the corporation. It was not the lack of insight or even of imagination that brought us to our present situation."

"What was it?"

"It's not a simple answer. First, Frank was a quiet man in leading a discussion, yet he was always available to anyone who wished to discuss something. He saw himself as a great delegator. 'I never do anything that somebody else can do,' he said. 'To do so is duplication of effort.' "

"How did it work in practice?"

"I think he was a great overdelegator. Frank made two flawed assumptions to justify his approach. One was that subordinates knew more about what was going on than they actually did. The other was that since they knew more about their situations they could therefore handle them better than Frank. The first assumption was wrong, or at least limited, because he didn't communicate well enough for them to know the big picture. The second was wrong because he needed to know about situations in order to exercise effective leadership. He justified his own lack of information by presuming the presence of that information at levels beneath himself. Basically it was the blind leading the blind. Frank thought it was the subordinate's job to pose questions to him rather than his job to focus issues with subordinates. As a result, you might say that he sat back and waited to react.

"In the beginning, that's the way things worked. Then as his subordinates got to know the score better, they discovered that when they asked questions they never got much help. So over the years they stopped asking. This was okay with him because he thought no news is good news."

"What did he do when subordinates did raise problems?"

"He countered by asking, 'What's your recommendation for handling it?' It became known around the corporation that if you were going to bring up a problem with Frank, you'd better have a solution that you're prepared to live with, and for good reasons. Frank would invariably say,

'If that's what you think best, why don't you go ahead and do it?' If you didn't have a good solution, he'd say, 'Why don't you think about it some more and come back when you do?'

"There was only one area in which he would take a firm position. If the action went over budget, he'd turn it down. Even then, when a budget barrier arose, he'd say, 'I wish the money were available for me to authorize it. When our situation improves, you may be able to move in that direction.'

"People soon came to realize Frank was giving them double-talk. They already knew when a budgeted item needed to be changed, and authorization for a change was the reason they were coming to Frank. He simply didn't examine the benefits of the decision and the bottom-line contribution that making an exception would make. The budget was his eleventh commandment. When the finance committee reviewed budget deviations above a certain amount, they would want to know why the expenditure was necessary. This was legitimate, but Frank must have said to himself, 'It's easier for me to turn down the budget deviation than to justify it.' I think he got a sense of personal security from living within the budget because he never had to face the potential censure of the finance committee for going over it. We were able to stay afloat and continue to look reasonably good because of the expansion of the total market, not because of good management."

"Would it be accurate to say that Frank was a passive leader?"

"That's the point. He did not exercise leadership. It would be hard to identify a single occasion in which he brought up something based on his independent thinking and analysis of our problems."

"Are you picturing an organization which was essentially headless for seven years?"

"I think that's a very picturesque way to describe it. We were drifting, doing the best we could in a market characterized by stiff competition. It's amazing that for seven years we've been able to maintain the same profit position we had at the beginning. It's partly because a lot of muscle was exercised from beneath the executive suite."

"That gives me a picture of a treadmill organization. How did Frank spend his days?"

"He enjoyed traveling a lot and being seen around the various operations. A trip was a presidential tour of duty. He didn't use visits to the field to learn, to correct problems, or even to get to know personnel. These trips may have provided escape from boredom of the twelfth floor. I didn't see any impact of these visits, but I assumed there was more to it than was visible from the surface. As you know, he was widely known as the 'man of silent steel.' I've always been a little curious about that description. A better term might have been 'man of silence.' "

"He must have had some way to put people at ease, or was he simply able to walk in, sit down, say nothing, remain for a period of time, get up, and walk out?"

"Oh, he talked. He enjoyed banter, and he was pretty good at telling jokes. Humor had the effect of filling time, entertaining people, and keeping them away from issues. He had a dry wit that drew people to him. He was a little bit of a clown. For example, at a field location he'd say, 'I sure would like to look around. Have you got a vehicle I could use?' Of course, there was no difficulty in satisfying that request. Then he'd say, 'I'm not so familiar with this place, so I think I'd better have a driver.' He'd say to the driver, 'Let's go down to the construction project.' Then, in his business suit, he'd put on a white safety hat and safety glasses, and the driver would take him there. He'd get out, walk around, saying little. Finally, he'd go up to somebody and say, 'Sure would like to help you, but I'd get in trouble with the union, wouldn't I, if I did any work?' That would bring a laugh. He'd saunter back, get in the automobile, and say, 'Let's look at operations.' So the driver would take him to an assembly area. He'd walk down the line and say nothing. Finally, he'd spot somebody and say, 'Sure would like to give you a break, but the union would break me if I broke the contract.' Sometimes he would even pat the person on the shoulder as he walked away.

"What do you think their reaction would be? They loved it. There was nothing in his remarks that conveyed a belligerent attitude toward the union. In a way he was kind of down on their level but always in his three-piece suit. These stories traveled the circuit, and he became famous as a 'character.' On numerous occasions, the plant manager would arrange for the photographer to snap this impromptu give-and-take. Then they'd send him a set of glossies. He always got a chuckle out of them, and the rest of us did, too.

"What did he learn from this? Very little. It occupied time, made him visible, and made him look colorful. It wasn't until I saw how the problems had piled up I realized how little was going on. The situation provides a perfect answer to the question of how a person can be present while absent."

"How did he spend his day at the office?"

"You can draw your own conclusions when I describe what he did. He arranged for his secretary to read the mail and bring to his attention those matters outside of her scope. I can tell you she had a pretty big scope, so to speak. He'd ask her, 'Would you get the information to answer this and draft a response?' When a matter arose that baffled her, he'd ask her to 'check with Barbara and ask her to respond, or help her if you can be of assistance.' Or, he'd give her a general statement that sounded good on the surface but might be hard to decipher."

"Could you give an example?"

"If he received a letter of complaint related to our products' falling behind, he might respond, 'While we are interested in advancing our product line through new designs, we are prepared to do so only when our customers can anticipate the same high quality from the new product as they have enjoyed from the current one.' He was implying that our competitors had moved beyond us at the expense of not validating the equipment they were producing. He would never, never name a name."

"What you're describing, then, is an effort to say something that really said nothing—an empty statement."

"Oh, yes. That describes him to a *t*. He enjoyed the cryptic motto. Ben Franklin had long since endeared himself to Frank in his 'a penny saved is a penny earned.' In marketing terms, he'd say things like 'We're like Darwin's turtles. We've found our niche.' Were anyone to venture a remark such as 'And we move at the same speed as Darwin's turtles, too,' that wouldn't disturb him. He'd say, 'Well, don't knock turtles. Some of them live for 500 years.' This suggested that we would, too.

"I may be straying, but this is the best I can do to answer you as to how he spent his days in the office. He enjoyed reading the *Journal*, or at least he read it, and he kept up with the *Financial Times*. He read *Forbes* and other business magazines. Beyond immediate business newspapers and magazines, he did not seem to have any interests in the trade journals relevant to our business. I believe that's about as far as I can take it. He was pretty hollow.

"I'll give you a bit of hearsay for whatever it's worth, though I can personally confirm it as more than just hearsay. Every once in a while people mentioned that they thought he changed the covers of some of the magazines he read. When you looked inside, they weren't about business at all, but were *Golf Digest* or *Sports Illustrated*."

"Any *Playboy*?"

"No, only the out-of-doors sports seemed to strike his fancy. One more thought: occasionally he closed his door. Of course, none of us interrupted when this happened, so I can't say what he engaged in during these periods. I know that in the right-hand drawer of his desk there were always six or eight Western novels. There may have been a connection between a closed door and the open prairie. The only other explanation is a nap. But I prefer the wide-open-spaces theory."

"I think I get the picture. Let me ask another question. Many corporate leaders hold convictions about their vision of the corporation. My question is, what did Frank stand for and how strongly?"

"That I can answer. He strongly affirmed what most of us believe in. For example, he frequently spoke of the role of free enterprise in an open society. He had thought this out in a thorough manner. He was not just mouthing worn phrases. He had at some time in life considered the role of government in either planning the direction of the economy or assuming a hands-off attitude. I think he was even a little bit extreme on this. He preferred to believe that the marketplace would catch misdeeds in the long run and that government's overseeing business through a regulatory approach was the greater evil. He harks back to the years prior to the New Deal, though I think his version of the good old days is somewhat romantic, as he wasn't there any more than I was.

"His own leadership was analogous to that of government in an open-market economy. He was operating a laissez-faire system, possibly under the impression that by doing so subordinates would exercise initiatives within their domains to create a livelier and more stimulating corporate environment. This analogy certainly is consistent with the manner in which he conducted his responsibilities. He stood for and lived by the credo that the less leadership the better."

"Even though you've described him as a remote person, he must have been called on to settle differences between subsidiaries or functions."

"You'd think so, but he wasn't. I cannot think of an example of any positive action in dealing with disagreements or disputes. The key was his tendency to make rules. When you study his rules, it turns out that they had the effect of freeing him from situations of conflict.

"When it came to meetings with the executive committee, neither of which were scheduled on a regular basis, he did not encourage give-and-take discussion. I have heard him say he saw executive committee meetings as update sessions. Each person came to update him on the status of things he needed to know for Board meetings. Since no colleague was an adviser to another colleague, there were few or no occasions for conflict. If someone wanted to follow up on what another said, this occurred afterward. Frank thought he was discharging his responsibility for developing subordinates because they heard each report. By listening, they could supposedly understand the issues under discussion.

"He had another rule, too, that'll add to the flavor of how he dealt with conflict. The rule was, 'When in doubt, ask for it in writing.' If he didn't really understand what was being said in a report, his request would be, 'Would you put it in writing?' It wasn't that he wanted to study it; it was that he didn't want to ask a question that would show his ignorance or provoke a disagreement. 'Put it in writing' was a way of exchanging information without probing deeper meanings or implications that might generate disagreement.

"Sometimes he still didn't understand the written report. Then he'd jot a note on it to say, 'Interesting. Thanks a lot. Could you elaborate a bit on the implications of what you say?' The word 'interesting' handwritten on a memo came to mean 'more work.'

"The avoidance of conflict by rule-making really did permit the passing of information without 'heat.' It kept him sufficiently posted to be able to deal with the Board, yet left subordinates on their own."

"By the way, I suspect what you've already described as overdelegation is another aspect of Frank's concern to avoid disagreement."

"Precisely."

"What about coordination? Undoubtedly there were important needs of coordination that must surely have merited the attention of the executive committee and that called for open interchanges."

"Not really. Subordinates had long since concluded that if they had coordination problems they'd better get together among themselves and find the solution rather than utilizing these higher-level sessions. That's what they did. It's not that coordination was all that great, because so many problems had fallen in the cracks."

"Are you saying there was little or no teamwork?"

"I think there was no teamwork that involved Frank Collins as the hub of a wheel or even that showed his influence on the company via a chief of staff. If anything, his chief of staff was his executive secretary. She occasionally offered thoughts on important matters, though in such a way as to be helpful rather than to assume responsibility for consequences."

"I'm still in the dark on one important issue. How were decisions involving Frank made?"

"That's a good question. Decisions were made, and I've often wondered how. The way I see it is that Frank hung back until the inevitable decision began to be evident. He then made it in an almost nominal manner. The exception came whenever he was sitting on a problem and a subordinate became so distraught by the delay that he faced Frank head-on and pleaded, 'Mr. Collins, your decision is absolutely required. It's costing the company a prohibitive amount to continue to study the problem.' Under these conditions, and possibly out of need for self-respect, Frank himself would come up with the least objectionable decision. This was decision making under severe pressure, and it's the exception."

"Let's move on unless you have other comments. What about critique?"

"None of it. He certainly was not a man to review the work of others or to engage in MBO, performance appraisal, or any other technique. Laissez-faire and critique are incompatible with one another. You can't leave things alone and also concern yourself with them, or so he thought."

"Was his resignation a surprise?"

"Yes. His memo read, 'Effective January 1, I intend to resign as president.' It was a pithy announcement, given without further explanation. I was in a meeting where people tried to ask him why. He relied on banter to divert attention from any thoughtful response. Someone said, 'But Mr. Collins, I thought you didn't fish.' He said, 'Well, I'm going to now.' We all knew that he didn't mean it, but it was an effective shutoff as far as further queries were concerned. He was a man of few words all the way. I suspect he was quite an unusual man to carry the reins of a large corporation so freely and for so long without getting into trouble. He simply did not have the interest in shouldering the task that has fallen on the next generation of corporate leadership."

"I'm somewhat surprised that he lasted until he chose to resign."

"Product development by his predecessor carried us through his first four years, and prosperity the next three."

"That brings to mind another question. I can understand Frank's elevation to president because of the precedent of promoting the next in line to that position when it became vacant. But I don't understand how, operating as he did, he ever got as far as executive vice president."

"Well, he rose through the ranks of the company because he hadn't operated that way. There was a time when he was one of the most respected managers in the corporation. He literally developed our southeast plant from the ground up and turned it into a showplace of the industry."

"What happened to him? What caused the change?"

"With his record and the outstanding performance of the southeast plant, he was the prime candidate for the executive vice president's position when his predecessor was promoted to president. Since our plant operations are basically the same, it was assumed that Frank as executive vice president could accomplish with the other plants what he had been able to do with the southeast plant."

"Did that prove to be overextended logic or wishful thinking?" asked Walt.

"Not initially. Things went well for the first year or so, just as they often do in a new political administration. But even though all our operations are similar, there are still differences. Frank had to contend with union problems in a couple of the plants. He'd never had that problem before. Some of the plants were trying to operate with antiquated equipment, and there was a considerable market shift to the west. Frank put forth tremendous effort, but the problems continued to pile up."

"Is that when he constructed the cocoon?"

"No, he was still in there plugging away. But by the end of his second year as executive vice president, it became apparent that the company's cash flow problems had become critical. The Board decided the company had to divest itself of some of the operations and generally tighten up on the others. Ultimately that meant selling the southeast plant."

"That," said Walt, "must have been a blow."

"More than just a blow. Frank had spent ten years at that plant. It was like a child to him, and as executive vice president he had to oversee the sacrifice. In the year or so before the president's death he gradually became more and more aloof from operations. Unfortunately little notice was paid because business began to turn around during that time. Then, of course, the president died, and Frank succeeded him. Somehow the new challenge just wasn't enough to compensate for his previous disappointments. I think he must have decided that by being uninvolved he wouldn't be subjected to those kinds of distasteful situations."

"How would you evaluate prospects for the future?"

"We have been coasting on product reputation while funds expended for research and development have shrunk for us and increased for our competitors," said Harry. "Now we foresee market loss. There's just no way we can maintain our competitive position, given the revolution that's going on in the whole area of materials handling. New methods permit materials to be handled by electronic equipment, operating in narrow aisles and increasing space for inventory. We are still marketing products of a decade ago. There's no way to avoid a period of hard times as we attempt to turn the company around."

"Do you think Frank foresaw that and preferred to resign rather than to live through the problems that will be encountered?"

"That's how I understand it. Seeing what was coming up for us and for the economy, he simply didn't have the strength to bring about the turnaround. He exited gracefully when he could."

SUMMARY

A 1,1 orientation may result from several possible factors, such as the Peter principle, burnout, or premature aging. It seems justifiable to conclude that a seniority system with bureaucratic rigidities, such as found in large corporations, family-owned companies, and government agencies, is more likely to promote a 1,1 style of leadership.

Motivations

The expanding market in prosperous times provided the favorable environment for Frank Collins to hold on to the chief executive officer position for seven years. He moved into the position primarily because of seniority and was able to avoid being at cross-purposes with the Board's financial committee by maintaining a "no-direction" budget cycle. He went through the motions, traveled throughout the corporation to add his presence, and leaned on direct subordinates to run the show.

The prospect of being unveiled in the near future and perhaps asked to leave when the company took a nosedive led him to resign.

Initiative

Frank's initiative was almost entirely stimulus-response. He overdelegated and compounded this by failing to stay informed. His expectation was for subordinates to bring him questions rather than for him to focus issues for them. He routinely turned problems back to subordinates for resolution. This stimulus-response mode was altered only when a crisis brought about the need for action.

The 1,1 approach to initiative is: "I put out enough to get by."

Inquiry

At best, Frank's inquiry was shallow. He read some general publications but made no effort to study trade journals relevant to his business. This shallowness is shown in his management committee meetings where he merely had update sessions to cover him at Board meetings.

The 1,1 approach to inquiry is: "I go along with facts, beliefs, and positions given to me."

Advocacy

Frank touted free enterprise and other values which he had come to accept over time. He transferred the notion that less government is better into less leadership is better. His uninvolvement in issues caused him to be known as the man of silence.

The 1,1 approach to advocacy is: "I keep my own counsel but respond when asked. I avoid taking sides by not revealing my opinions, attitudes, and ideas."

Conflict Solving

Frank's approach to conflict was to be neutral or avoid it. He created rules so that he would not find himself in conflict situations. Examples were his update sessions, in which give-and-take discussions were discouraged to prevent conflict. Another tactic was to ask for reports in writing both to disguise his ignorance and to avoid having to ask questions that might provoke disagreements. His overdelegation was another means of conflict avoidance.

The 1,1 approach to conflict solving is: "I remain neutral or seek to stay out of conflict."

Decision Making

Decisions were made basically by default or by delegation. His strategy was to sit on problems until the decision became inevitable. When faced with a situation of crisis proportions he would act, taking the least objectionable alternative he could find.

The 1,1 approach to decision making is: "I let others make decisions or come to terms with whatever happens."

Critique

He did not employ critique and feedback. This was consistent with his idea that the less leadership the better. To have employed critique would have meant involving himself rather than leaving things alone.

The 1,1 approach to critique is: "I avoid giving feedback."

Adverse Consequences

> Frank relied on subordinates' recommendations and offered little to solutions beyond authorizing their actions (pp. 106–107).

When subordinates come to realize that the person above them is operating as little more than a figurehead, for all intents and purposes, there is a headless organization. If people do not naturally pull in the same direction, the corporation is pulled and pushed according to subordinates' more limited perspectives.

> Frank's budget was his eleventh commandment. Whenever an item requested was over budget, he denied it, regardless of its merits (p. 107).

When the budget is sacred, the corporation comes to exist for the purpose of satisfying the budget, rather than allowing the budget to provide a basis for sound planning and orderly execution. Such a policy sacrifices opportunities needlessly. The ends and the means have become confused.

> Frank took trips to visit field locations for no apparent reason other than to escape boredom (pp. 107–108).

With this way of killing time, a leadership void ensures that needed decisions will not be made but, rather, deferred. Others' time, which may be in short supply, is wasted for no apparent gain except personal gratification.

> Whenever faced with an important decision, Frank deferred action by asking for a further report in writing (p. 110).

This way of dealing with issues, which on the surface may appear to be a way to ensure thoroughness of proposals, can be a cover-up for procrastination or deferral. A further report in writing is not likely to generate improved understanding of the issue. It may be a way to prevent the leader from exposing his or her own ignorance, but it may do little to advance the solution to the problem at hand. It might smoke out the casual proposal for which the subordinate has little convictions, so that the extra effort of writing is justified.

> Frank used meetings to update himself rather than to study problems or promote the free flow of ideas necessary for solving them (p. 110).

While updating is a valid purpose for a meeting, it can also be used as a time filler and a way of avoiding other more demanding communications. When team members are seen as little more than information terminals, their potential for deliberation is being short-circuited.

Overview of the 1,1 Grid Style

That the 1,1-oriented leader has little interest in either production or personnel does not imply a dull or lifeless individual. Rather, it is possible for a person actively to pursue many interests and pastimes outside the context of corporate life.

The 1,1-oriented person usually desires to stay in the organization and goes through the motions of being an executive. Some leaders do this well by fulfilling ceremonial expectations and carrying out executive duties with flair, even though there is little truly personal in such events. Their observable behavior conforms to requirements of the job description and affords protection by making them unnoticeable. This means being on time and in place in the executive suite; displaying an unperturbed, studious attitude; avoiding early departures; fitting vacations to others' convenience; and promptly responding (or arranging for others to respond) to correspondence and memos. These actions give the appearance of involvement.

Retaining a low-key and colorless presence frequently avoids provoking undue resentment. "If you don't say much, they'll never ask you to repeat it" depicts this approach.

A stream of remarks may give the appearance that the executive is saying something. Many leaders are skilled in using a lot of words to say very little. "One-liners," stories, reminiscences, and anecdotes all take conversation time and serve to amuse listeners.

SUGGESTIONS FOR CHANGE

Many times a leader has drifted into the 1,1 orientation without realizing it. The following suggestions offer ways of reestablishing direction and purpose.

Motivation

1. Picture the kinds of changes that would permit you to snap out of the 1,1 orientation.
2. If you find yourself saying, "Why bother? It doesn't matter," reassess your degree of uninvolvement or indifference. Is this an enjoyable way to spend eight hours a day, or would you find greater satisfaction from strengthened commitment?
3. You might examine the personal consequences of being terminated. It is always possible that a 1,1-oriented leader is riding for a fall, and you may not have drawn this possibility into focus. Thinking it through may be enough to reactivate doing a better job of leading.
4. Many who have slipped into the 1,1 corner or who have gotten there via burnout have discovered they do not like what they see upon self-diagnosis. The contrast between what they admit to be true and what they wish to think about themselves is sufficient for rearousing interest and involvement.

Initiative

1. You may see ways to take actions, since you probably possess consider-able skill in exercising initiative when you are motivated. It's more a matter of will than skill.
2. You might talk with your Board. Ask for more assignments.

Inquiry

1. Asking more questions of subordinates is invaluable in rebuilding your knowledge base.
2. Pick up pertinent literature, articles, and news reports. See what they have to say. Use them for further inquiry with subordinates.

Advocacy

1. Answer in a straightforward way when someone asks a question.
2. If asked questions on topics you haven't thought about for some time, give the questioner your pledge to investigate. Set a time to do so. Keep that schedule.
3. Take positions so that others know where you stand.

Conflict

1. Stop taking mental walkouts when people disagree. Explore and resolve differences. This is an important step toward establishing a stronger basis of teamwork.

2. Avoidance of disagreement is less rewarding than a meeting of minds. Others are usually ready to go more than halfway to find a mutually acceptable basis for resolving disagreements.
3. Others may seem to disagree with you because in the absence of clear-cut statements from you they must make assumptions about what you think. If you have not stated your convictions, get them out into the open where it is possible for others to disagree with them.

Decisions

1. You might answer the following question before you hand a project over to someone: "What can I do to help get this project completed in a successful way?"
2. You may see how to involve several subordinates in solving many-sided problems. Coordination may strengthen the practice of sound teamwork.

Critique

1. Once you have started doing things on your own initiative, this may be the time to get feedback. Ask subordinates. Give them straightforward readings on how you see productivity, creativity, and so on. Overall productivity may increase through working together as a more closely knit team.

10

PUSHING
ALL THE
RIGHT
BUTTONS

"Let's pick up the story as of three and a half years ago," Dave Rivera, the human resources vice president, said to Walt. "At that time the Board appointed a search committee to fill the chief operating office slot. After six months they chose Don Henson. He had been an executive vice president in another company with similar manufacturing facilities and was known as a 'whiz kid.' After he and several others had been interviewed, he charmed everyone, and from then on the choice was Don, hands down. For a company of our size, being president at forty is almost without precedent. The dramatic turn of events came six months ago when he was fired. Although the reason given for his resignation was 'policy differences,' the fact is he was booted out. That's what brought the promotion policy under reexamination. The Board is about to reach a decision, and I'm pleased with their conclusions."

"Yes," said Walt, "when I spoke with the chief executive officer he was appreciative of your report on executive selection. He suggested I might find it useful to talk with you and I'd like to go into some of the details. How did you do it? What's it all about?"

"Well, I'm sure you know it was triggered by the situation with Don. That has been a dramatic affair. Something of an explosive ending to a meteoric career. As might be predicted, he's still on his feet and doing well."

"I know the story only from the outside," said Walt. "I'm sure there are many significant twists and turns that have yet to be uncovered by the press."

"There sure are. Don is the tip of the problem, and my project was to get to the bottom of it and offer suggestions and recommendations for dealing with it."

"How did you go about it?" asked Walt.

"I contacted my counterparts in the other companies where Don had worked and got them to set up other interviews so I could get to the facts on a firsthand basis. Fortunately, I've been active in the personnel societies and networks. I've created a lot of entrée by attending meetings, getting to know people, giving papers, preparing articles, and so on. So, I had no difficulty in setting up interviews.

"As a result of this overall study, the Board is considering shifting to a promotion-from-within policy. In the past, whenever a vacancy arose, the question was 'who is the best person anywhere to take on this responsibility?' A large number of those at the top of our company have come from other businesses. The new policy would be a significant shift from a free market basis of open selection to a more planned basis for selecting and developing executive talent."

"How did Don go from being everybody's to nobody's preference?"

"Don Henson," explained Dave, "was known by those who worked under him as cold and ruthless, out for Number 1. He took credit for their accomplishments and put himself into the limelight with those above him."

"Did the search committee not check his track record out, or did you in personnel not follow up sufficiently?"

"The former possibly, but not the latter because we weren't directly involved. This was such an important assignment that the CEO wanted to handle it as a personal matter. But how many subordinates of prospective candidates for managers are ever interviewed?"

"Not many."

"That's one of the keys. Recommendations are usually sought and given from a person's boss or colleagues, not from subordinates! In this case the search committee requested recommendations from executives in four previous companies, all of whom were pleased to be called on. Our CEO took advantage of their availability, and I don't fault him on that. He did a good job of digging out information they could provide.

"Now back to my project. Once I knew what I was looking for, here's what I found about how Don got his reputation. He had a keen knowledge of the levers of power. He constantly brought himself to the aid of seniors, sometimes two or three levels above himself. Through his own boss, he let them know he was willing to do anything or go anywhere to help them— take special assignments, be an errand boy, get information for them, or assist with special reports. He's smart as a whip and was able to deliver whenever asked to do something special. These people knew his value to them, and he sealed the deals by being lavish in praise of them. He practiced being a protégé—a fair-haired type to these older men. He came to be known as a star. According to my investigation, he befriended five different seniors over the years, and it was these people whom he made look good. He never took credit for what he did for those above him. This is in contrast with his taking personal credit for whatever subordinates did under his leadership."

"How did he do it? Was he a con artist?" asked Walt.

"No. That's the interesting part. He succeeded by delivering those things he had already figured the senior person wanted or needed. When he couldn't find a need he could satisfy on their behalf, he'd try to create one. He might say, 'It seems to me the company should have someone get to know more about the Japanese ways of managing. I don't know anyone more qualified to do that than you.' When the executive would say, 'I've never been to the Far East,' Don would answer, 'Is that so? I'm sure you would find it interesting.' Three months later, the target person would be on the way to the orient with Don Henson carrying both briefcases. From that point on, the company had at least two Japanese experts.

"It doesn't take too much talent to succeed in such terms; you just need to be ten, twelve, or fifteen years younger, work your heart out, and constantly laud your target senior to one and all inside and outside the company. Don, moreover, not only did all of the things I've said, but was a press agent and a public relations man thrown in. He was admired by those whom he befriended. They invited him to parties, and he was as charming to their spouses and friends as he had been helpful to them. He saw to it that the wives got greeting cards on anniversaries, birthdays, and holidays. Wives can be cheerleaders, too."

"What about colleagues—people of Don's rank? What was the situation there?" asked Walt.

"People of similar rank didn't think of him in the same way as his seniors, but they didn't despise him, either, like his subordinates. He used several tactics with colleagues. One was to do favors that created obligations, and he created needs in them, too. When a favor didn't work, he was not above using a little leverage; for example, he might imply readiness to use information that would be embarrassing if made known. He never used it, so he never got a reputation for telling tales; but he left an innuendo here and there, particularly when he was sure it wouldn't backfire.

"There are other aspects, too. Don almost never had a meeting with more than one other person, and that's without regard for whether the person was above, below, or beside him. By knowing a person pretty well on an individual basis, he could then shape a request or directive according to that person's needs."

"If he was that kind of a man, how did his subordinates view him?"

"He pressured, bullied, pushed, and drove those who worked for him. He tolerated no disagreement. He watched them closely and constantly, knew more about what they were doing than they knew themselves."

"Did they become his enemies?"

"No," replied Dave. "With subordinates he appealed to fear, but only when necessary. He threatened without appearing to be demanding. He made it clear he would give them loyalty in exchange for their loyalty, but theirs had to be proven first. The proof of loyalty was to do whatever was asked, to come up with whatever was demanded, to put in endless and extra hours, to be on top of detailed information, never to be caught napping at the switch, and so on."

"Did they become enemies of one another?"

"That's harder to answer because the situation was not so clear-cut. But he was not above saying to one subordinate, 'Look, Bill, you've really got to buckle down if you want to catch up with Fred.' Five minutes later he'd say, 'Look, Fred, you've got to turn on the juice if you want to stay up with Bill.' The Freds and Bills became aware of one another and sometimes felt threatened, but they really didn't know why. They never found out Don was pitting them against one another. He was quite a behind-the-scenes operator."

"What you've described is giving different strokes for different folks," observed Walt. "For some people the stroke was a petting response, pleasing to them; to others, it apparently was a painful one, punishing; with still others, Don created obligations. That's a complex way to operate. I can imagine his behavior was inconsistent from one person to another. Did people catch on?"

"I don't think so," said Dave. "He was courteous in all this, praising people and expressing appreciation for those who did something of use to him. You get the picture—he knows everyone's name, is friendly, warm, and ready to applaud and appreciate."

"Most people use one approach or the other. How did he work out the contradictions in his own mind?"

"You have to remember that Don's motivation was to be Number 1, and everything he did was geared to coming out on top. By being a protégé to people higher up, he won their approval and, incidentally, their recommendations for his advancements. By being helpful to colleagues he gained their acceptance. While he had juicy morsels that he might have used to discredit them, he rarely if ever did, and they almost always appreciated his not doing to them what he might have done. The odd thing is he had everyone doing something for him without his requesting or even demanding it. They wanted to do it either to increase their own sense of personal prestige, get on his inside track, or to reduce their own anxiety.

"Many subordinates were threatened by him, but their lips were sealed by his harping on loyalty. His first commandment was, 'I can help you only after you help me.' He also made it very clear that when subordinates talked with people outside their group, they were to speak well of it and support it with the highest enthusiasm. 'No dirty linen in public' was the way he put it.

"But there's a quirk of human nature in this, too. Some of them said, 'Beat me harder. I can take it. Let me prove myself.' Of course, he was only too ready to oblige."

"I wish you'd get to the other end of the story, and tell me why he got canned. Did he have his hand in the till?"

"No, so far as I can figure out, he never did a crooked thing. He never dropped over the line into dishonesty or truly underhanded or underworld dealings. He was more an actor, exploiting situations, but within the boundaries of ethical constraints. I'll get to the reason in a minute. In the meantime, do you have a feel for what Don was all about?"

"I think I do, at least as far as motivation is concerned. You're telling me he wasn't a facadist, but I have no earthly idea as to how he succeeded."

"There are several different answers to that. That's the key question the CEO was interested in, once I began explaining it."

"Okay," said Walt. "A part at a time. What's part 1?"

"Well, let's talk about teamwork. Don attended formal meetings to hear firsthand the speeches and pronouncements of key people. He was not a dominant participant but listened to the debates attentively. Then he studied them. Just when the meeting was drawing to a close or before a decision was finalized, he would step in with a summary of key points under discussion and possibly identify emerging areas of agreement. In this way he owned the problem and its solution. Many people got in the habit of waiting for his summaries to pull it all together. Later on people would call on him to do this. Each summary added two or three points to his IQ.

"He didn't get caught up in disagreements or take sides, either. Many times he could rise above them and present an alternative that resolved the issue. Frequently, he'd wait till after a session and approach different individuals with proposals that each could buy. In this way, he was unlikely to get caught in the hot action but earned a reputation for being able to manage or help with tough situations. By the way, he didn't get at loggerheads with the important people either. He'd find some way to give agreement or support without appearing to contradict himself in the process."

"How did he conduct meetings?"

"It sounds a little difficult to believe, but he rarely had any problem-solving meetings with subordinates. He usually called people together to ask advice, but it was a sham. The session was a good way to probe them for information, opinions, and so on. He had meetings to make announcements. He dealt primarily with subordinates on a one-to-one basis when he needed to get things done.

"The other part was how he gathered information and was in the know. Consistent with what I said earlier about using leverage with colleagues, Don undoubtedly knew more about whatever job he took and about what was going on throughout the organization than anyone else. He knew every potential target: the competitor's or helper's age, serial number, sexual persuasion, quirks, appetites, pleasures, needs, habits, weaknesses, drinking problems, drugs, what he or she did on company trips—the works."

"But how did he gather such a wealth of information? What did he do with it when he got it?"

"He studied every person like a book, not only for what they knew about a given problem or how they would approach that particular problem but also how they thought, with whom they were friendly, by whom they were antagonized, and what they thought of other people.

"When he couldn't get information by asking questions directly, he gleaned it from third parties. He was a genius at using parties of the second part as windows to see parties of the third, fourth, and fifth parts. He enjoyed listening to subordinates of other bosses talk about them. In clever ways he was able to get them to talk without appearing to interrogate. Many people like to complain or talk to a sympathetic listener. Somehow or other Don had an unusual knack of getting people such as secretaries and chauffeurs to open up and reveal themselves about a target person two or three levels up the organization. He had an uncanny ability of getting a person to open up by finding his or her tension points and appealing to them, but no one saw how he did this because he did it in private conversations."

"In other words," said Walt, "he made himself an intelligence agent and not only developed information but also kept his own inventory and made use of it in forwarding his career."

"And," continued Dave, "as he learned more and became more indispensable to those above him, he would mention job opportunities in the company or get his friends to bring his eagerness to serve to the attention of those at the highest levels. When this did not bear fruit, he'd say, 'It looks as if my career in this company is blocked,' and send his mentor a different request. It would say, 'I've been contacted about a position in company X. While I'd hate to leave, I can't afford not to give it every consideration. Can I ask for your help by requesting a letter of recommendation should that be called for, or will you speak in my behalf should you be contacted?' They were honored. That's how our CEO got outfoxed in the first place. Doting parents are as eager to advance the careers of their adopted children as they are of their own flesh and blood."

"How was he contacted by these outside companies?" asked Walt.

"Through a search firm," replied Dave.

"Did this become known in the firm where he was working at the time?" asked Walt.

"Never."

"How come?"

"You've put your finger on another clue to the mystery," said Dave. "The fact is that he had a fifteen-year continuity with the same executive search firm. Along with his lawyer and his accountant, he saw them as a part of his support system. The more he worked with them, the more they knew what they could do for him. The search firm was his gatekeeper through whom his future superiors got glowing reports from his current superiors."

"Oh, I see. It's now beginning to come through. I imagine these senior persons would hate for him to leave but on the other hand felt a personal indebtedness for what he had done for them."

"That's how he worked it, but they gave him more than positive recommendations. They gave him an A+ report card.

"All this leads into another angle," continued Dave. "While he was always seeking information, he was not an open source to others except as he was able to stand for things that resounded to his credit. He avoided taking a stand on controversial issues or ones that might throw him on one side or another of a disagreement. He commented on the events of the day—national or international, political or nonpolitical—in such a way that he was not seen as radical. I doubt anyone knew for certain whether he was liberal, moderate, or conservative, yet he knew political leaders in all factions. He did stand for the verities—profit, quality, service, reliability, and steadiness of purpose. He was a weather-vane executive. The only stands he took that were unpopular with subordinates and colleagues were ones that his bosses wanted and which, by giving them his commitment, demonstrated his loyalty to them. In such circumstances he'd say, 'Sorry, but this is what we've been asked to do.' "

"You've led me up to the point, but you haven't sprung the punch line. How'd he blow it?"

"Well," said Dave, "actually he blew it twice, once here and once a long time ago, just a few years into his career."

"How did that happen? And why didn't it affect the decision to employ him here?"

"I'll be as specific as I can, but unfortunately some of my information about the early days of his career is sketchy and secondhand.

"He advanced rapidly in a division of a large, decentralized manufacturing firm after receiving his undergraduate degree. I don't know this for certain, but I would suspect he was able to do so using the same methods he employed elsewhere. In any event, he eventually became the top assistant to the division director. In this job he served as liaison with the plants. There were five of them in widely scattered locations. As you can imagine it was the kind of position Don played to the hilt."

"I can readily see that. Did he try to assert himself over the plants?"

"No, he wasn't that ambitious at the time, or perhaps he was just more cautious in those days. Anyway, to make this as brief as possible, Don decided that the division needed to undertake something unique to raise its prestige in the eyes of the corporation. He quickly found out that there wasn't much to be done by way of improvement at the plant level. Their equipment was modern, management was sound, union relations very good, and performance levels high. So he turned his attention to the division central staff operations. He discovered that, while the manufacturing facilities had complete quality and quantity indices and reporting procedures, staff operations had little. So he persuaded the division director that if similar performance measurement and reporting systems could be installed in central staff operations, it would be a first in the corporation and a way to increase the division's prestige at headquarters."

"On the surface that sounds like good initiative and creative thinking."

"On the surface, yes," replied Dave, "except there was no bedrock underneath. Neither Don nor anyone else at central staff knew how to design and implement such a system. Don was given the assignment of working with a consulting firm to develop one for central staff. In his haste to install the program Don made two critical errors. The people who were to implement the program were not consulted prior to its installation. That in itself created a lot of unhappiness and resistance. The other error was that the program was inappropriate for the kind of work done by central staff."

"In what way?"

"Well, the program was what I call a paper management thing. I don't recall the exact name; it had one of those clever acronym titles. Basically the problem was that it was geared to routine, generally repetitious tasks, of which there were few in central staff. It also involved quite a bit of paperwork, recording times for specific jobs, rating output against pre-established standards, and so on. Just managing the paperwork associated with the program began to consume an inordinate amount of time."

"Was the program scrubbed?" asked Walt. "Or did it just die a natural death?"

"Neither. It had been the division director's decision to implement the program, and because of its expense—a significant percent of their operating budget—he was reluctant to give up on it easily. But pretty soon the effects were beginning to be felt at the plant level. When plant managers began howling about poor support from central staff, something had to be done. The program was reduced to a shell, with only lip service being paid to it."

"What was the impact on Don when the eruptions started?"

"The division director had to take responsibility for the program, and he had to take a lot of criticism from both central staff and the plants. But he surely didn't need to be reminded on a daily basis of how he had been taken in. I'm convinced he made this clear to Don, although I don't know exactly how it happened. Anyway, Don's resignation was promptly forwarded along to headquarters. His stated reason for leaving was to return to the university for an advanced degree, and that's what he did for two years prior to resuming his career."

"When you think about it, that's a pretty clever way to cover your tracks while recovering from a pretty severe blow."

"True, and since the division director was so embarrassed at being drawn into the fiasco, he kept quiet about it. By the time we became interested in Don many years had passed, and that blot on his record was all but gone. Incidentally, I have only recently uncovered this information from a friend of mine who worked in that division for a short time. From what she has told me, most of it has now taken on the character of war stories and legends from ancient history, so there's probably no way ever to determine all the details accurately."

"To return to recent history, what brought about his demise here?"

"Well, as best I can dope it out, he had the problem Harry Truman said no president should let happen. He had the-buck-doesn't-stop-here problems when he became president. The way it worked out is that the CEO had been phasing himself out of senior responsibility by expecting others to exercise authority without his constantly giving agreement or support. He expected Don to formulate plans, to stand behind them, and to do the homework that made his arguments plausible. Don took off like a rocket and made dramatic and showy decisions. The Board had given him carte blanche, and the chickens came home to roost. One decision was a costly merger, but he was unable to get it all together. He had presumed the takeover would be a friendly one, but Don's company was seen as a black knight and by the time the shark repellents and resistances had been worked through, the deal was too expensive. All of a sudden, he wasn't doing something for someone else and had to shoulder the responsibility, for worse, when the merger failed. He had to stand on his own two feet and act in his own name. That had an exaggerating effect on his self-doubts. I think the number 1 problem he had in corporate life was in setting direction by his own initiative. When he could pick up somebody else's formulation or act in someone else's name and help move it along, he was fine, at least in the sense of being seen as competent.

"It sounds too simple an explanation, but he tried to make the CEO into the chief executive as well as chief operating officer. The CEO wanted nothing of it, because he's a funny guy himself, a loner. Nobody can sneak up on his blind side or butter him up easily—the kind of stuff Don was brilliant at. Another quirk of fate: the CEO didn't go for one-on-one conferences, either. So Don couldn't study him in private or figure out what he wanted and then deliver the goods.

"The CEO wanted full responsibility in the hands of the president rather than having to make decisions that Don could run with. So you might say that Don's problem was decisiveness. He was immobilized when he had to stand or fall on his own decisions. In my book this is what caused the firing. He couldn't buck decisions up to the CEO; yet he didn't have the stamina and strength to reach decisions regarding the company's destiny. Whereas all through his career he had been known as confident and decisive, he was now seen as procrastinating, stalling, and resisting the responsibilities expected of him. In spite of all of his bounce and projected self-confidence, he was ridden by self-doubt. When things went sour and his responsibilities for them became evident, he went into a nose-dive. When, after four years, that kind of leadership pattern had become the rule, the CEO decided Don had to go."

"Did he go quietly?" asked Walt, "Or did he put up a fight?"

"He went quietly," said Dave. "The settlement wasn't bad, and, lo and behold, you know what he's doing now? He's a hotshot consultant, really making it in his own way and in his own time, and the job fits. As a consultant he can be helpful while avoiding the trauma of decisiveness."

"Did you find this Don-type problem in your interviews with other firms?" asked Walt.

"This is the first time I've come face to face with this problem," answered Dave, "so I can't say. In conversations within and outside the company I've found a growing concern with Don's kind of opportunism, that is, career jumping from one company to another to gain personal advancement, often at the expense of the new employer. This concern also has shot down the CEO free market concept of personnel selection. The slogan 'May the best person win' has been replaced by 'How do we develop the best so the company and the individual can win as a consequence of personal contribution?' Now, as far as we are concerned, we intend to apply attention to what a manager is doing for the company rather than for himself.

"The implication is that this particular search firm was working for Don more than it was for us. It looked to us almost like collusion. Last week the CEO got the search firm's principals in and reviewed the entire story. I was present. He put it on the line, saying, 'This is our parting of the ways unless you're prepared to pledge your allegiance to us as your client rather than to your candidate as your client. We have the need. We pay the bill. You are working first on our behalf, not the candidate's.' "

"What was the reaction?" asked Walt.

"I'd call it a very sobering conversation. It took an unexpected twist. They were as much in the dark about how they were being used as anybody else. They felt that Don was a talented man, as proved by his apparent success before he came here. The discussion ended by someone's joking about the Peter principle, and it was agreed that in his present role as a consultant he does have a lot of potential. Therefore he is not an example of the Peter principle. It was only when he became the president that he couldn't put his finger in the dike."

SUMMARY

Motivations

Don Henson's motivation as an opportunist was to "get there first," and to take whatever actions or project whatever images were necessary for him to become a statesman, hero, or strong leader later. His actions were calculated as a means to personal gain, and his leapfrogging from one corporation to another and always landing at a higher level reflected his primary concern.

The opportunist's positive motivation is to be preeminent because the top gets the limelight and gains one attention and glory. The opportunist seeks to avoid actions that might result in being a face in the crowd or being dropped to a lesser position.

The difference between this and other leadership orientations is that the objective is not to make the corporation better, but, instead, a selfish one, to become Number 1.

Opportunists expose their Achilles' heel when they have no option but to act in their own names and shoulder personal responsibility for consequences.

Initiative

Don exhibited a high level of initiative in ingratiating himself with his seniors, doing favors for colleagues, and closely supervising subordinates. He expended prodigious effort in his quest to be Number 1 even to the point of creating a previously unfelt need in a boss. He provoked his boss's curiosity about Japan in order to promote a trip there, and then of course Don went along to help. Earlier in his career he had used similar tactics in persuading the division director of the need for a performance measurement and reporting system.

Inquiry

Don's inquiry was thorough. He made it a point not only to know the job and organization inside out but also to know in detail as many qualities of the people he dealt with as possible. This included searching for likes and dislikes of superiors and weaknesses of colleagues, knowledge of which might give him leverage. He used second parties to glean information which might be useful to him but about which he did not want to risk open and forthright inquiry. The purpose of such "intelligence" work was to formulate strategies for advancing himself, however.

Advocacy

Don's advocacy of any issue depended on the person with whom he was dealing. He avoided taking a stand on controversial issues although he gave lip service to profit, quality, and other values that are not subject to debate in the corporate world. Basically, his convictions parroted those of persons with whom he was dealing, particularly superiors.

Conflict Solving

Don's approach to conflict was to avoid taking sides or getting into disagreements. Rather, he tried to present others' ideas in such a way as to appear to be their author. At times he negotiated separately with contestants in order to appear supportive. He suppressed subordinates' disagreements by charges of disloyalty.

Playing on others' individual quirks and needs is a reasonable means to corporate advancement only if you presume that everyone else also is asking, "What's in it for me?" With the motto "Different strokes for different folks," Don could appeal to others' love, fear, greed, and avarice to maneuver them without overt conflict and with a minimum of resistance.

Decision Making

Don's style of decision making varied, depending upon the situation. He planted ideas in the minds of superiors both to advance his own aims and also to compliment them on their sound judgment. When dealing with colleagues, as in meetings, he waited for a decision to begin emerging before involving himself. In this way he could take credit for a decision that others had come to support.

Don's subordinates were subjected to unilateral decision making. However, when finally put on the spot of making decisions on his own, he was trapped. He could no longer play off others' ideas, and there was no way to diffuse responsibility.

Critique

Don employed no systematic use of critique as a learning mechanism. Feedback to others took on the character of compliments and praise for superiors and criticism of subordinates.

Adverse Consequences

> Don pitted subordinates against one another competitively in order to increase their productivity (p. 122).

Unquestionably, competition can spur great effort and generate outstanding results. However, pitting one subordinate against another can create almost inevitable hostility and uncooperativeness, with each subordinate distorting information about the other. When cooperation is needed, it is then unavailable. Seeing antagonisms and invidiousness between subordinates, the chief executive is likely to attribute these consequences to "bad chemistry" between them rather than to his or her own behavior, which stimulated the rivalry in the first place. Executives who fan the flames of destructive rivalry are not likely to recognize their destructive impact because they view themselves as the intermediary through which the benefits of cooperation can be marshalled.

> Don listened in meetings in order to summarize emergent areas of agreement so that he would receive credit for the ideas (p. 123).

The self-appointed role of summarizer is undoubtedly one of great power. The summarizer is likely to become identified with the solution and often is in the position to take credit for it even without having contributed to its formulation.

The summarizer role is doubly powerful when played by a subordinate who, like Don, wants to advance up the corporate ladder. By not actively participating in the open discussion, Don kept himself out of adversarial relations with others who inevitably fell into disagreement among themselves. He was there to pick up the pieces.

In time, lateral colleagues come to resent summarizers because they realize that others are taking credit for what they are contributing. While summarizing is indispensable, the usurper of others' ideas serves to weaken teamwork rather than strengthen it.

> Don approached individuals separately to gain their
> concurrence prior to presenting proposals in a later
> one-to-all meeting (p. 124).

By approaching individuals separately to gain concurrence, a leader can appeal to the personally vested interests of each. This kind of sociological consensus leads to inevitable agreement because the leader has predetermined that everyone will ratify the proposition. Unfortunately, it also means that the participants themselves are predisposed to serving their own selfish interests rather than viewing the problem from a corporate perspective. Innovation and creativity may come from a more free-wheeling approach, in which each person is encouraged to examine a problem from many points of view and to contribute by bringing forth reservations and doubts which, if evaluated, might make the proposal an unacceptable one.

> Don used others to learn about third parties
> (p. 124).

Some executives listen to what second parties think about third parties to build up a fund of information more for surveillance than for assessing managerial talent. Such information includes preferences, prejudices, and personal quirks, that is, what makes the third parties tick, at least as viewed through the eyes of second parties. The information allows the leaders to develop a reservoir of data about third parties without their awareness of it.

When subordinates become aware of what is happening, this kind of surveillance promotes a general attitude of wariness, reduces openness, and increases suspicion and distrust. Such an atmosphere can eventually heighten the readiness of members to work for selfish or vested interests rather than in behalf of corporate interests.

> Don made others dependent on him not only through
> satisfying existing needs but also through creating
> needs in those whom he wanted to make dependent
> (pp. 121–122).

The manipulation of people's needs for the benefit of one's own selfish interests is a questionable approach to effective management. Over time, people become aware that they are being manipulated and build their defenses, thus leaving the manipulator in a weaker position for exerting constructive influences than he or she might otherwise have occupied.

PERSONAL STYLE CONSIDERATIONS

Opportunism is a mixture of Grid styles. The executive's particular mix depends on his or her experiences of what styles yield the best personal results. Every action is for tactical reasons and serves as a means to personal advancement. The key behavior is to get into a situation first and then clean up one's act to project whatever image will make one look like a statesman, hero, or strong leader. Thus, simple sentence descriptions are inadequate to portray each of the facets of opportunistic leadership.

Many opportunists avoid actions that might result in being just one of the crowd. They may seek to be in the limelight, whether at a party or in the Board room. They move to the center and draw attention to themselves. They are the star.

Reading others' personal motivations, needs, and desires is the key to operating as an opportunist, whose belief is that everyone has selfish interests that can be appealed to or vulnerabilities that can be threatened. Vigilance about who is saying what to whom, who is on the fast track, or who has the inside advantage helps the opportunist answer, "What's in it for me?" This premeditated inventory of knowledge about people and their relationships puts the opportunist in position to take advantage of their strengths and to avoid being entrapped by them. The executive who uses leverage to elicit cooperation or threatens to expose a raw nerve is said, depending on whose side is joined, either to be able to manipulate people, or to be a skilled negotiator.

The opportunistic executive is one whose strong feature is to think ahead, plan, and always to have a contingency in mind to grapple with whatever may happen. When uncertainty or indecision arises, the opportunist takes the initiative and rivets attention on his or her prefabricated answers to what to do. Such use of contingency plans may have genuine corporate benefits, but it is stimulated more by the personal advantage to the executive for getting ahead or staying on top.

SUGGESTIONS FOR CHANGE

An opportunist faces two kinds of key problems in trying to develop greater effectiveness through corporate contribution. One is a shift in fundamental values regarding production. The shift is from viewing production as a means to personal gain to seeing it as an end in itself because what is produced meets the needs for goods and services and of the corporation for profitable operations. Furthermore, the management of production can be a gratifying activity in the sense that solving problems that impede productivity is itself a rewarding experience; problem solving challenges one's ability.

Likewise, the opportunist must shift values associated with people. Achieving results with everyone, the leader included, involved in and committed to the success of the enterprise is far different from regarding the shoulders of others as steps to one's own advancement.

When a leader sees productivity as a positive value and bosses, colleagues, and subordinates as capable of involvement and commitment to corporate success, a shift from opportunism to a more effective leadership orientation is feasible.

11

MANAGING
BY
LEADING

"Let me start by asking you to review Angus McMillan's career, since he has been retired only a short time," said Walt.

"Okay," said Chris Bruback. "Angus came into the corporation on an acquisition. His training had been in engineering, but he had previously been president of the acquired company, founded by his father. Their main business was government defense contracts; so as a result, this acquisition provided us entrée into government business.

"As a result of these circumstances, Angus was the youngest man and the only outsider reporting to the president of the parent corporation. Then the chairman and president retired. It was natural that we all rallied around Angus. He seemed to have a broader picture. He was finally designated as the CEO, ostensibly because he had top executive experience as head of his own company, even though it was small. But I think it was more than that. The Board sensed that only he could keep the top echelon together and get the company going in one direction."

"Well, it's widely recognized this is a well-managed company. At least that's the outside reputation. Does that square with how you view it from the inside?"

"Yes, and it's because of the corporate culture that Angus hammered out in his years of leadership."

"Did you know Angus well?"

"Well, our careers were in tandem over a thirty-year period. He had the chairmanship; I was head of the research laboratories. So I knew Angus very well. We were more than colleagues but less than close friends or confidants. Our relationship was based on mutual trust and respect, but that's not really different from most relationships he had."

"It would help if you would freewheel a bit and give me your reactions as to the kind of leader he was."

"He saw managing as leading, no question about that. He was always trying to lift up a particular problem or situation in order to see the management principle beneath it. His notion was that if we could see the premise on which an action was based and then test the principle underlying it, we could see how to solve that problem and others like it.

"Whenever a problem arose, his question, which we all in turn came to ask, was 'What principle of sound business logic was disregarded to cause this problem?' Or he would ask the question the other way around: 'What principles of sound business should provide the operational architecture for this company?' "

"Isn't this an abstract approach, unrelated to reality?"

"No, the other way around, actually. Our think tank was concentrated on real-life problems that would do us in if they weren't solved or would block us from seizing a new opportunity if we didn't have a solid basis for approaching it.

"I think he revealed one of the characteristics of his leadership in a question he posed every once in a while. He asked, 'Who works here? Are they just people? Are they individuals? Do we think of them as bodies or hands?' We'd say, 'In a way they are all these things, but if we don't go beyond, we miss the fundamental point. They are members. They aren't employed by the company; they have joined it. If they haven't joined the company, it's our fault. When people feel membership, they are already identified with our purpose. This situation is ripe for involvement and commitment, loyalty, and dedication. Without those membership feelings, words such as *teamwork* are a sham. With those feelings everything is possible.' "

"In terms of this emphasis on thinking, where did Angus get his ideas?" said Walt.

"He was articulate, and he was an avid reader. He could deal with a wide variety of topics, get others involved in them, and benefit by the discussion. He didn't build a wall around himself. He was constantly on the move: visiting the field, consulting, reviewing, engaging others in critique. He expected the rest of us, too, constantly to study the corporation and its people. He learned from study and investigation and from critique, review, and feedback. I think his almost total openness to new ideas and new problems, geared to finding underlying principles, is what gave him greatness of leadership."

"You've mentioned management-by-principles several times. Perhaps we'd better concentrate in that area for a moment. Could you come up with an illustration of what you mean by a principle?" asked Walt.

"Yes, I can. His Number 1 principle is purpose. Organizations exist to achieve purposes. If the organization purpose is unsound, unclear, or nonexistent, the organization is on the verge of trouble. It's out of purpose that meaning comes. Out of meaning, motivation is derived. This principle provides the spur to move forward to greater effort.

"He returned again and again to the same conclusion when examining the purpose principle: in a capitalistic society the ultimate purpose by which an organization measures its effectiveness is return on investment or assets. Of course, he used "return" in a broader sense than many use it. He meant an optimal return. We didn't operate to maximize return if we priced ourselves out of a market or created a niche a competitor could fill. Also included in his concept of return was that not only the stockholders but also the employees and consumers got an optimal return on their investments. That entailed both products and people of good quality. He used the word *integrity* for both product integrity and people integrity and he meant the same thing in either application. His fundamental dictum was 'We are a value-creating organization. If we fail to put value into our products, we fail our customers, our sources of finance, and our people. Customers buy a product because they want the value it contains.' "

"Was this emphasis on purpose limited to him, or was it more widespread throughout the organization?"

"Decentralization, which was functional in character, was the way in which this concept came to life through the company. Decentralization was his principle of organization structure. Any decentralized component can be evaluated for what it is contributing through a return on investment assessment, too. When that can be done, there is a basis for investment decisions.

"Another example is a purchasing policy which was also evaluated in this same general way. When one segment of the company supplied a product to another segment, it had to produce and price it as if it were selling to a noncaptive buyer. This way the producer did not lose money, and the buyer had no phony basis of gain. This internal use of purchasing policy between components was critical because within an integrated company such as ours, it made each organization component stand on its own feet.

"I've given these examples as though there were absolute policies; however, another aspect of his mode of thinking was the view that nothing is absolute. There were special circumstances when an intracompany transfer might have been made at less than published prices, but they were unimportant except to know they existed. Internal transfer prices competitive with open market pricing is a more widespread arrangement these days, but the idea was quite an innovation when he introduced it and he also got us to buy it as a part of measuring return on investment."

"Having a built-in measuring device is a more widely appreciated idea these days. Was return on investment his sole criterion?"

"No. I should have mentioned it earlier when I brought up the idea of financial measurement in the first place. There's another principle equal to it that provides a guidance system for growth of the corporation.

"Angus was persistent in getting us and the Board to think through the concept of the nature of the business. Actually, the effort took several years. When he picked up the reins, the company was rapidly moving in the direction of a conglomerate. He focused on this question as a high priority agenda item, put people to work on it, and worked with them on it. He and many others became convinced that there's a lot of wisdom in the idea that we can't be all products to all markets. To do so, he felt, was economic opportunism. After it had been thoroughly thrashed through, the notion that emerged was that of synergistic growth around a central core.

"What that has meant," Chris continued, "is we built in high-tech prowess as the core concept of our firm and then let products related to that core find their way into different but interrelated products supported by a core marketing strategy, a core research and development strategy, and so on.

"The value of this to me was that as the head of the research laboratories it provided a definition of how to orient our research.

"This core concept has been effectively used in conjunction with return on investment. Two questions always were asked when a product proposal, a new marketing strategy, or whatever, was brought to the surface: 'Does this business activity fit the core concept?' If the answer was yes, then it had to stand the return-on-investment test by the proposing organization's footing the bill and adding it to the expense side of their ledger. If a proposal didn't fit, this didn't mean an automatic turndown if the proposing component had strong convictions regarding the idea and was prepared to persist. Rather, it led us to reexamining the core definition and asking the second question: 'Have we narrowed our field of endeavor? Should it be expanded, shifted, or modified?' This concept has remained viable and is becoming even more so since the high-technology world is now moving more rapidly in our direction."

"Are there other benefits to the core concept principle?"

"Yes. We can build a cadre of technically competent people. By mobilizing our knowledge resources across divisions and components, we have successfully resisted duplicating people."

"Do you have worries about the concept's being too confining?"

"No. I don't think I've seen all that many limitations. We constantly probe how well conglomerates are doing just to test whether we are outsmarting ourselves. I think we've seen a good number that went in the conglomerate direction and overextended themselves, getting into business areas without the technical competence for operating the subsidiary. I have in mind Exxon's buying Reliance Electric, (in other words, an energy company's moving into motors). General Electric got out of their effort to combine an electric manufacturing company with a mining company, namely Utah International. We've watched American Airlines move out of the hotel business, and we've observed the troubles Mobil, an energy company, had in trying to relate to the retail business of Montgomery Ward.

"I don't think the final chapter on the core-versus-conglomerate argument has been written yet. All I can do is give you the conclusions we've reached. They're based on a number of hard decisions and critical choices that have stood up well."

"How did Angus go about getting people involved on such a level of thinking and study about the corporation?"

"In a number of ways, but I'll concentrate on two because both reflect the same basic approach. He advocated strongly for the need for a conclusion rather than the conclusion itself. The difference may not be immediately clear, so let me explain. Time and again I've heard him say, 'Does this company need to reach a conclusion on a real estate policy?' or 'Do we need to come to a conclusion on remuneration policy?' or 'Does this company need to develop a policy for technical engineering standards?' The subsequent discussion centered on what was meant by 'the need to reach conclusions' on any particular policy. As the need became clear in the minds of those who debated it—members of Board committees, line and staff personnel, as well as divisional representatives— the importance of the policy became more and more evident. Once they became committed to why it was needed and what it would contribute, half the job was done. It was then possible for Angus to take direct responsibility, with the Board and with top management groups concentrating on personnel policy, use of return on investment, and nature of the business. In time, he deployed others in developing and recommending policies, but always with Board approval.

"Let me come back to the pricing policy. It was hammered out in operating divisions by joint committees, with each division committed to the policy position finally recommended. Angus got the best thinking from committee members who, incidentally, were most aware of the finer points leading to the decision. Also, he earned their commitment to making effective use of the policy once it had been finalized.

"I might say he had a thorough understanding of the meaning of involvement and commitment. Since I've already emphasized the significance he attached to clear thinking, it's important to note he had as much respect for the thinking of others as for his own and wanted their input before final positions were reached. He got their involvement and commitment at the outset, not just at the application or implementation level. I think that's of importance in understanding the strength we've achieved and have been able to maintain."

"Has this emphasis on involvement and commitment always been a facet of his leadership?"

Chris hesitated briefly. "Well, yes and no. Yes in the sense that I believe he always had values that were more or less congruent with the notion of involvement. However, in the beginning it had more of a hit-and-miss character. He was always an energetic type, one of those who tends to stay ahead of others. In the early years he made a number of decisions, valid for the most part, that did create some unhappiness and footdragging. It was difficult for him to understand at first, but he finally came to realize that people were not resisting his decisions but rather the way in which he had made them. He came to see that leading involved more than pushing or pulling. Once he came to be more systematic about involving others, the positive results reinforced his convictions about it. He fell off the wagon a number of times, but that happened less and less as the years went by."

"This might be a bit of a divergence, but it would help to understand how what you've said thus far affected the operation of the research laboratories," said Walt.

"Well, we had to come to terms ourselves with these policy positions and their implications for everyday activities. This led to a number of sound developments. Once we achieved understanding of the core concept, we determined to concentrate our research activities to adhere to that principle. That's difficult to do in the abstract; so coordinating committees from the different operating divisions served to assess various research areas and projects so as to get the greatest payout from the research dollar. What we would do with these recommendations was our ultimate decision, but the user organizations' assessments brought concreteness to what can be a pretty abstract process of decision making. In terms of internal costing policy, whenever we took on a project which was for one user only, then, of course, we charged the expense back. Also, when the research would have mutual benefit to several users, we distributed the expenses among them. This very quickly let us know the extent to which the users thought they had benefited by our contributions."

"Were the users free to go outside if they could get the research done more cheaply? In other words, were they as free to buy research competitively as they were when buying products interdivisionally?"

"Yes. But again, every policy has exceptions, and this one did, too. The corporation didn't want users going outside if it meant sharing new technology we wanted to retain. Other than that, though, they were free. We studied the proposals to ensure that they were bidding on a comparable piece of research, and we reviewed the outside research organization's reports for our own education and also for judging the quality of their work. Except for these limitations, it was the same policy all the way around—something of a what's-good-for-the-goose-is good-for-the-gander approach."

"I'm curious about how Angus dealt with conflicts. There must have been many vested interests at work."

"Surprisingly few, and I've often wondered about that myself because I've not had corporate experience elsewhere. I've heard that some companies live with protagonists in constant battle."

"How do you account for its relative absence?"

"Angus's emphasis on thinking is part of the reason. Another is the emphasis on grappling over a policy before moving into its details. It's really quite amazing. When people convince themselves a need exists, it is much easier to resolve differences by compelling logic rather than by pecking order or that sort of thing."

"What happened when conflict arose?"

"I can give you an example of what happened in our top team. Angus would get the principals together and say, 'Look, I realize we have important differences here, and, while differences are desirable, they can also be impediments. I want to get to the root of why we have these differences and see if there are solutions to them.' He'd always have the protagonists present, and they'd stay with it until he felt they understood. If they continued to have blind spots, he would work with them until they had been removed. He believed that intelligent people in a reasonable frame of mind should be able to look at the same facts and reach similar conclusions. If not, there was a problem of communication, further inquiry, or some cause other than 'chemistry' that one needed to identify in order to get rid of it. He expected us, in turn, to face up to the conflicts that existed in our own teams and from time to time reviewed with each of us the main battlegrounds in our shops and what we were doing about them.

"Not everything worked out so well. Once there was a stubborn type who couldn't seem to reach a meeting of minds with anyone. While he could intellectually subscribe to many of our principles of involvement, participation, and teamwork, he was never able to do so at the gut level. At the first strain or difficult situation, those principles went out the window. After a year or so with him at the center of constant hassle, he had to go. Angus had no difficulty facing the inevitable conclusion."

"You mentioned that Angus studied, traveled throughout the corporation, and reviewed and critiqued extensively. What you've described up to the moment seems informal and impromptu. Did he have a more formal approach?"

"At the end of each year all of the senior people, including division heads and their teams, and the principal Board members met at some retreat location," answered Chris. The retreat started with review of the total corporate operation in order to find explanations for why things took place the way they did, by relating them to the external business environment, significant market trends, competitors, and so on. Then each division went through the same procedure, but in the presence of the headquarters group and the Board. As a result, by the end of two weeks everyone from division level up was fully informed as to the health of the corporation for the previous year; weaknesses were pinpointed, and recommendations for grappling more successfully with them in the year ahead were made. This proved the highlight of the year because it enabled everyone to identify with the corporation as a whole and gave divisional leaders a sense of close corporate identity as well."

"How would you describe Angus's motivations? What made him tick?"

"I suppose," said Chris, "that the word *dedication* captured his underlying value system. He identified with the company and took great delight in seeing it prosper. He also suffered personally when part of the company confronted difficulties. He never stepped away from difficulties or brushed them off by saying, 'That's their problem.' When others seemed to have difficulty getting solutions, he was likely to appoint a task force from each of the several divisions and put them on the project to find out how they would solve it as a thinking group, with each coming at it from his or her own divisional experience. If a division leader experienced repeated difficulties, then it was another matter and had to be faced as a personnel problem."

"You mentioned Angus's dedication. I wonder how you would answer this question: was he a workaholic?"

"No. I think the man had an excellent perspective on himself, the corporation, and the larger society. As a matter of fact I know when he left the company, he left; he didn't take it home with him. He was not one of those 7:00, 8:00, or 9:00 p.m. guys who walked out with two briefcases and came back in the morning with puffed eyes. It was rare to see him carry papers home. He had an interesting philosophy on that, too. 'If we concentrate attention on the basic issues and not on curing symptoms, then eight hours a day should be more than enough to do a competent job of it.' I believe he was right, too. The idea that you have to put in a fifteen- or eighteen-hour day looks like real dedication on the face of it, but it may be a self-defeating dedication, too. I suspect one of the consequences is the high level of divorce and corporate suicides, to say nothing of heart attacks."

"I'd like to ask a final question. How did Angus respond to compliments and recognition?"

"It's true we have an outstanding record in terms of return. We've been able to establish an outstanding reputation for product quality and for an attractive dividend to stockholders. In addition, we have an outstanding remuneration program and retirement plan. Those things are good, but to concentrate on them is to see them as outcomes that have been produced by the kind of corporate leadership I've described and the character of the corporate culture that has unfolded as a result. They all come together: top leadership, corporate culture, and the bottom line are different ways of looking at the same thing.

"But he took compliments and recognition in stride. He was a selfless character with no need for fuel to power his ego. He's chuckled to me once or twice after the Board's year-end appreciation banquet, 'They think I'm the one who did it, and if I deny it they think so even more.' So he tried to take public acclaim in stride and accept it in good grace with a bit of humor."

"I have a better feel now for how the company looks from the inside point of view," commented Walt, "and it really is much different from what you learn in the press."

"Oh, I recognize that," said Chris. "The press deals with bottom lines, major debacles, and things like that. It's difficult not to get a narrow perspective."

SUMMARY

The 9,9 type of leadership presumes a necessary connection between organizational needs for production and the needs of people for full and rewarding work experiences. The leader's desire is to contribute to corporate success by involving others so that they too may contribute. Such a can-do spirit is contagious, inspires a winning attitude in others, and promotes enthusiasm, voluntarism, spontaneity, and openness.

Motivations

Beyond the description of typical 9,9 leadership motivations in Chapter 4, Angus also exhibited a strong desire, which reflected his value system, to help people feel membership in the organization and a sense of dedication.

Initiative

Angus took strong initiative to formulate a strategic model of the corporation and to engage others in effecting it. Being a leader rather than just a manager was a constant theme in his actions and in his efforts to see that others operated in the same manner.

Inquiry

Angus seemed to personify the meaning of "study." He was an avid reader and enjoyed engaging others in discourse on a variety of topics. He studied the corporation in a thorough manner, both in its operations and in its people. His openness to the ideas of others undergirded his style of inquiry.

Advocacy

Angus held strong convictions. For example, he constantly advocated the concept of management by principles and persisted in having corporation members and the Board examine the elements of a strategic model, key financial objectives, and the nature of the business. Because of effective inquiry he was both thorough and articulate when conveying ideas and concepts.

Conflict Solving

Angus addressed conflict by seeking out the elements contributing to its presence and essential for its removal. He tried not only to specify disagreements but also to isolate them and study their components. In this way he might identify the causes of conflict in lack of inquiry, poor communication, or other defects. But he was unwilling to permit conflict to cause disabling impediments or to accept it as due to "chemistry."

Decision Making

In the area of decision making Angus displayed a commitment to the principle of involvement. This permeated his thinking, from decisions regarding the overall corporate model to specific issues such as pricing. He spared no effort to bring others into the decision-making process and to discuss issues fully with them in order to get understanding and agreement.

Critique

The use of critique was an Angus hallmark. He used critique on a regular basis even to include such areas as core definitions of some aspect of the corporation. The yearly meetings were a formal and exacting use of critique to learn about and improve the business.

VARIATIONS IN THE 9,9 STYLE

At one level of analysis it might be said that Angus McMillan and George Thomas are different from one another, and yet both have been characterized as examples of the 9,9 style of leadership.

Their differences are illustrated in any number of ways. George Thomas had a sense of urgency, but Angus McMillan had almost the opposite: an eight-hour day, no homework, and so forth. The Thomas tenure seems to have been more heavily laden with conflict than was true for McMillan, even to the point of firing a manager fifteen years his senior for insubordination. McMillan's leadership was characterized by a lesser degree of conflict than might have been expected under normal circumstances. McMillan's style of inquiry differed from Thomas's. He asked, "Do we need . . . ?" whereas Thomas asked, "What's the score . . . ?" These and other distinctions set the two men apart.

At another level, however, we realize that these differences are variations on the 9,9 theme. Both men were propelled in the direction of serving the corporate whole, something larger than themselves. They contributed to it rather than taking from it. Neither was out to pick up accolades or to build a reputation for himself.

The leadership elements can be compared on a one-by-one basis, but the important thing is the pattern in which the elements come together. Given the differences, both were active inquirers. Thomas was more oriented to specific problem solving than McMillan, who asked, "What's the general case of which this is the specific example?" Both were men of conviction who wished others to know their thinking, and both projected a clear vision of the corporate future. Neither had reluctance to face conflict in an operational and candid way, but Thomas seems to have been blunter and more provocative than McMillan. Both regarded delegation and decentralization as important means of making operational decisions where the needed information was readily available. Delegation was also a means of giving people responsibilities under conditions where they could effectively practice leadership. Finally, both took advantage of critique for learning how to improve on past performance, though McMillan may have been more deliberate in doing so, as exemplified by the formal and rigorous year-end meetings attended by top corporate personnel, as well as division-level management and their teams. This pattern of teamwork, in which interdependence among key personnel, reinforced by open, free, two-way communication, was the rule. It promoted the likelihood that markets could be recognized and penetrated; quality products developed, replaced, or upgraded to meet emerging needs; and future leadership planned for as a renewable resource.

The leadership strategy practiced by the two men bore the same stamp of a 9,9 style. What varied were the tactics of application, determined by factors unique to each situation.

LEADERSHIP IS ASSESSED BY ITS CONSEQUENCES

Why the 9,9 style of leadership can make such a positive contribution to the bottom line is described below.

Impact on Productivity

Several conditions together ensure productivity at a high level. A positive culture is created when participants have clear goals, thorough knowledge, and strong convictions candidly expressed. Thoroughgoing conflict solving, effective decision making, and in-depth critiquing ensure the fullest utilization of human resources.

Impact on Creativity

Creativity, particularly with respect to synergies possible from effective teamwork, also emerges at a high level. Energetic initiative means the assessment of many different approaches for solving a problem before deciding on final action. Thorough inquiry ensures the maximum likelihood of fully identifying real problems rather than accepting shallow definitions. Clear expression of convictions means that members get their ideas out into the open where they can be challenged, corrected, or used. Conflict solving permits participants to have differences and, through open confrontation, to avoid personal antagonisms. Using critique provides the possibility of learning to increase effectiveness.

Impact on Satisfaction

Contributing provides satisfaction. Many more opportunities to participate in meaningful ways make for important differences in personal and corporate performance. Satisfaction is likely to be long-lasting.

Impact on Career

The superiors of 9,9-oriented individuals evaluate them to be the most reliable and capable persons to advance the interests of the corporation. Research evidence confirms that maximum rate of advancing within an organization is characteristic of those who manage according to a 9,9 orientation.[1]

REFERENCES

1. Robert R. Blake and Jane S. Mouton. *The New Managerial Grid*, Gulf Publishing Company, Houston, 1978, pp. 204–206.

12

ORGANIZATION CHANGE

The leaders described in this book have depicted a variety of Grid styles. Most of them are limited in one way or another, but two are of unusually strong character. One of these was George Thomas, who shifted the entire direction of his company into one of high productivity and profit sustained over the long term. The other was Angus McMillan, who created one of the strongest companies in America.

All of these leaders, Thomas and McMillan included, exercised leadership based upon assumptions about how leadership should be exercised. For the most part, we can imagine that these assumptions were not arrived at deliberately but rather reflected ways of thinking that had been learned earlier and on which they had come to rely. It follows that if their learned assumptions had been self-defeating or self-limiting, they might have replaced them with stronger assumptions had the opportunity been afforded them.

This chapter is concerned with how leaders may strengthen their leadership by recognizing their current assumptions, contrasting them with alternative assumptions, making appropriate conversions. Those who already exercise leadership have the option of bringing this kind of strengthened leadership into widespread use.

The Grid is a theory-centered approach to development in which change strategies are based upon learning to think more systematically about how to behave effectively and to gain personal insight into concrete actions to enhance one's own effectiveness. When change is viewed in this manner, it becomes self-evident that the culture of one's own company is also made up of operational habits, many of which have come into use in an unthinking or unsystematic way. These continue to be employed not necessarily because they are sound but because they typify the way things have been done in the past. Thus, the Grid approach rests upon (1) aiding all managers of an organization to examine Grid styles first in personal terms that clarify the current ways in which he or she is trying to achieve production with and through people, and (2) helping them learn the skills necessary for applying sound behavior to solving the major problems of organization. When this has been accomplished, many other opportunities develop which otherwise would not have been as readily available to the organization for strengthening its overall effectiveness. These basic steps and the other phases of Grid development are briefly commented upon below.

GETTING STARTED

How is Grid development introduced? How it is done is a major factor in its success.

Steps for Getting Organizationwide Grid Development Under Way

The first dilemma is in finding a way to achieve awareness among all members about the importance of Grid development without demanding participation. Ordering members to take part in development is close to a 9,1 way of operating and violates the underlying principles. A better approach is a series of exploratory steps designed to orient members to possibilities. These steps permit the organization to test the implications of Grid development without the obligation to become deeply involved. When the organization takes these steps in a planned way, members have the opportunity to assess their own commitments through a series of self-convincing experiences. Orientation without obligation creates the opportunity to produce awareness of possibilities on which to make a conviction-based decision. Some steps and activities include the following.

Background reading. Gives an orientation of how applied knowledge of human behavior can strengthen organizations.

Seeding. Provides information to a few organization members about the Grid seminar without necessarily committing the organization to fuller participation.

Pilot Grid seminar. Provides a test-tube trial of what would be involved were the organization to engage in in-company Grid seminars.

Grid OD seminar. Gives a few key managers insight into the whole of Grid development. Their evaluation determines recommendations for next steps in the program.

Pilot teamwork development. Affords the top team an understanding of the benefits from applying the Grid for strengthening its team effectiveness. Based on their own experience, participants can assess the probable impact of Phase 2 team building, applied on an organization-wide basis.

Steering committee. After these steps have been completed, an OD steering committee is appointed to consider and implement strategies and tactics for long-term organization development. It is a committee with heavy top-level line involvement to oversee the entire effort. Leadership is centered in line personnel, but it is important that the steering committee also include pertinent staff who can provide support for the entire effort.

Once a decision has been made to move forward, the Phase 1 activity is Grid seminars.

Grid Seminar

In the initial phase of organization development everyone in the organization is involved in learning about the Grid and using it to evaluate personal styles of managing. This involves attending a five-day seminar.

Maximum impact is possible when all employees who manage others take part, though some companies have extended participation to include technical, wage, and salaried personnel.

The seminar has four major goals:

1. Increase self-understanding by
   a. Learning the Grid as a systematic framework of thought, analysis, and comparison
   b. Gaining insight into how others describe one's own Grid style

  c. Increasing personal objectivity in self-critique of one's work behavior

  d. Reexamining personal managerial values

  e. Developing a common language for communicating about behavior throughout the organization

2. Experience problem-solving effectiveness in teams by

  a. Examining the need for active listening

  b. Experimenting with and revising ways to increase team effectiveness

  c. Studying the use of team critique

  d. Developing standards for openness and candor

3. Learn about managing costly interface conflicts by

  a. Studying barriers between teams

  b. Examining conflict within teams, and the origins of distrust and suspicion of other teams

  c. Exploring ways of reducing or eliminating such conflicts between groups

4. Comprehend organization change implications by

  a. Understanding impact of work culture on behavior

  b. Gaining appreciation of Grid development and how it can be used

These seminars are based on thirty or more hours of self-directed study before the seminar week itself, which usually begins on Sunday evening and runs through the following Friday. During the seminar, participants take part as members of learning teams that solve projects, study how they performed, and consider how to improve.

A valuable point of seminar learning is the other members' critique of participants' performance. Another is the managers' critique of the dominant style in the organization's culture. A third is the participants' concentration on steps for increasing the effectiveness of the whole organization.

As commented on in Chapter 3, a major barrier to change is self-deception. It can be seen in the following way. Prior to attending the Grid seminar, managers evaluate themselves by choosing Grid paragraphs to describe their personal managerial styles. During the seminar each participant receives written feedback from his or her colleagues concerning dominant and backup Grid styles observed in the participant's problem-solving and decision-making behavior during the week. The feedback is in the form of paragraphs describing specific and concrete behaviors illustrating the elements of initiative, inquiry, advocacy, and so forth. Then the participant reranks the Grid paragraphs selected prior to the seminar, to fit a new assessment of his or her dominant and backup Grid styles.

As shown in Table 12-1, a large shift, particularly away from the 9,9 Grid style, occurs between the first self-assessment and the second. Prior

Table 12-1   Self-Ranking of Dominant Grid
Styles, Pre- and Post-Seminar

| | Self-Rankings of Dominant Grid Style, % | |
Grid Styles	Preseminar	Postseminar
9,9	67.9	16.5
9,1	10.7	36.8
5,5	18.9	41.5
1,9	2.2	4.2
1,1	0.3	1.0

Source: Robert R. Blake and Jane S. Mouton. *The Managerial Grid III*, Gulf Publishing Company, Houston, 1985, p. 182. Reproduced by permission.

to the seminar, 67.9 percent of the participants see themselves as having a 9,9 orientation. After the Grid seminar only 16.5 percent see themselves as managing in a 9,9 way. How can this reduction of 51.4 percent be explained?

Better understanding. Higher standards of sound management are developed through better comprehension of the Grid's concepts, which makes it possible to be more objective.

Self-deception. A person who looks inward is likely to misjudge. One looks at one's intentions. Most persons have good intentions that correspond generally with a 9,9 orientation, but they are unlikely to recognize their actual behavior, which often is contradictory to good intentions.

New data. When people receive feedback from others on their behavior, they learn previously unrecognized things about themselves. With new information, they can see themselves more objectively and thus are motivated to change in the direction of more effective behavior.

Phase 1A

An important aspect of sound development work involves engineering how to apply seminar learning in a direct and organized way back on the job. These specific applications are spoken of as Phase 1A. The points that have been learned are applied to the organization itself.

Phase 1A activities may involve the formation of project teams or other work groups charged with the responsibility of solving problems or capitalizing on opportunities. In most cases the membership of these teams have been through a Grid seminar. One specific example is a data processing organization providing services to financial organizations. The organization decided to reduce the operating costs of several significant computer applications. In the past the top person issued an edict, including deadline dates. Instead, the organization decided to handle this project as a Phase 1A activity. Several work groups were formed and asked to employ the Grid skills learned in Phase 1 in a way that would achieve the objective. Each was also given the opportunity to evaluate the objective itself to make sure it was clear and that each person agreed with the need for achieving this particular cost-reduction target. The project occupied two months of part-time effort. The net result was that the objective was exceeded by a factor of 2½ and that operating costs of the various data processing applications involved were reduced by over $500,000 per year, computed in 1980 dollars.

Another example of 1A activity involves a plant in which the managers and staff members were in the process of Grid development. The plant manager assembled these individuals and reviewed with them a specific problem in the plant. Small work teams were formed, with the charge to formulate ways in which the problem might be solved. Again, the character of such projects and assignments is different because they are based on effective behavioral skills that were learned in Phase 1.

Managers routinely report that Phase 1A activities are successful because participants return from the Grid seminar energized and enthusiastic about applying their Grid learning to produce concrete improvements for the company.

Phase 1A activities either involve problems or opportunities within one department or, as mentioned earlier, may cut across the fabric of the entire organization. Other examples of typical Phase 1A projects include the following: setting new standards, forming work groups to find ways of reducing maintenance costs and small tool expense, and merging two departments into one.

The importance of 1A is that it utilizes the energy, enthusiasm, and learning derived from the Phase 1 Grid experience and enables participants to focus on specific projects that result in measurable benefits for the organization.

Team Building: Phase 2

Phase 2, team building, comes after Grid seminar participation and 1A project applications. Its purpose is diagnosing specific barriers to sound teamwork and identifying opportunities for improvement within actual work teams of boss and subordinates.

The goals are to:

1. Replace outmoded traditions, precedents, and past practices with a sound team culture.
2. Increase personal objectivity in on-the-job behavior.

3. Use critiques for learning and for improving operational results.
4. Set standards of excellence.
5. Establish objectives for team and individual achievement.

Central to Phase 2 concerns are issues of problem solving and decision making, when 1/0 (one-alone), 1/1 (one-to-one), and 1/all (one-to-all) solutions are needed (see Appendix). However, many more facets of teamwork are explored in depth. These include each team member's reactions to the contributions of others, assumptions about what constitutes effective teamwork, identification of particular barriers to effectiveness within the team, and specific plans to remedy them. Setting team objectives for future achievement is the final activity. Follow-up in three or four months is a useful additional step.

Team building can begin when all members of any management team have completed a Grid seminar and are ready to apply Grid concepts to their own team culture. It is initiated by the person in charge and those who report to him or her, and it moves downward. Each manager then meets with subordinates to repeat as a team the activity of studying barriers to effectiveness and planning ways to overcome them.

Grid team building typically is a several-day activity which is usually implemented during working hours. The activities can be segmented into parts and conducted over a longer period if this is necessary or desirable.

Interface Development: Phase 3

The third step is to achieve better problem solving at interfaces between groups through a closer integration among those that have working interrelationships. The need for Phase 3 development activities comes about when a department, unit, or division concentrates on its own assigned responsibilities without consideration of the effect on total company performance or its relations with other units. People may act and react in the interests of their department but neglect the interests of the entire organization. This is viewed from inside the department as selflessly serving the corporation, but such preoccupation may mean that less attention is paid to other departments than is needed to produce cooperation and coordination. The second department may ask, "Why are they dragging their feet? Why are they unable to provide the service we need, which is the only reason for their existence in the first place? They are deliberately ignoring our requirements."

The goals are to:

1. Use a systematic framework for analyzing barriers to interdependent cooperation and coordination.

2. Apply problem-solving and decision-making skills for the following:
   a. Depolarizing antagonisms.
   b. Confronting relationships based on surface harmony or neutrality that hide problem-solving difficulties.
   c. Resisting compromise when differences cannot be solved in this manner.
3. Utilize confrontation to identify focal issues needing resolution.
4. Plan steps for achieving improved cooperation and coordination between units with scheduled follow-up.

The importance of an integrated approach to development becomes evident when the extent to which the industrial world is segmented into divisions is recognized. The splits are manufacturing and marketing, personnel and operations, central engineering and the plants, operations and maintenance, and so on. The intent of each of these separations is to improve the utilization of personnel and to assign competent specialists to deal with the problems in the segmented components. However, there is a need to integrate corporate divisions, for no particular understanding of issues from all sides can be presumed. The heavy price of separation is misunderstandings, distrust, suspicion, lack of coordination, empire building, and so on.

An integrated approach makes possible redesigned subsystems so that a coherent basis of organization is available for strengthening overall performance. This is one purpose for interface development as the activity of Phase 3.

Interface attitudes of frustration can quickly turn into feelings of mutual hostility, rooted in mistrust and suspiciousness. These are easily provoked and, once formed, become win-lose power struggles. When this happens, needed cooperation is sacrificed, information is withheld, requests are perceived as unreasonable demands, and so on. When members are asked what their problems are, they tend to answer, "Poor communication." However, the underlying problems of distrust and suspiciousness at the interface must be resolved before fundamental changes in effectiveness of communication can be brought about.

Phase 3 is undertaken only by those groups in which actual barriers to effective cooperation and coordination exist. It is not a universal phase in which all groups automatically take part. Locally, interface development usually is undertaken after Phase 2, team building, has been completed, but some interface problems may be so acute that earlier attention is warranted.

Phases 1 through 3 make important contributions to corporate excellence, but none are sufficient for reaching the degree of excellence potentially available from the systematic development of business logic. The key to exploiting organization potentials is in the organization's having a business model of what it wishes to become in comparison with what it currently is or historically has been.

After completion of the first three phases intended to reinforce effective behaviors, the last three phases can be undertaken with greater likelihood of success. These last phases examine and attempt to strengthen the fundamental business logic of a firm.

Designing an Ideal Strategic Organization Model: Phase 4

The top team is situated to examine its current business logic and reject whatever is outmoded and unprofitable and formulate a replacement model. The new model requires the organization to define its future business activity according to the needs of society for products and services; of the corporation for profitability; of employees for security and satisfaction based upon involvement, participation, and commitment; and of stockholders for a meaningful return on funds.

The goals are to:

1. Specify minimum and optimum corporate financial objectives.
2. Describe the nature and character of business activities to be pursued in the future.
3. Define the scope, character, and depth of markets to be penetrated.
4. Create a structure for organizing and integrating business operations.
5. Identify development requirements for maintaining thrust and avoiding drag.
6. Delineate policies to guide future business decision making.

The top team studies, diagnoses, and designs an ideal corporate model in a step-by-step examination of business logic. The study is an intellectual investigation of the most basic concepts of business logic currently available. These are drawn from the writings of executives who pioneered in the development of a systematic discipline of business logic.

Using concepts of pure business logic with which it is in agreement, the top team takes the second step of specifying the operational blueprint (planning) for the redesign of the corporation. Phase 4 is completed when this strategic corporate model has been evaluated and agreed to by the next layer up and approved by the Board of Directors.

Implementing Development: Phase 5

Phase 5 is designed to implement the model and plans developed in Phase 4. It is unnecessary to tear down the whole company and start from scratch to meet the requirements of the model. What is done is more like remodeling a building according to a blueprint. Architects and engineers study the existing structure to identify strong and sound features, consistent with the blueprint, which should be retained; antiquated, inappropriate features that must be replaced; and usable features that need modification or improvement to bring them into line with the blueprint. Phase 4 develops the blueprint; Phase 5 identifies and implements what must be done concretely to shift from the old to the new.

The goals are to:

1. Examine existing activities to identify gaps between present operations and future operations in accordance with the ideal strategic model.
2. Specify which activities are sound and can be retained, which are unsound and need to be replaced or abandoned, and what new or additional activities are needed to meet the requirements of the ideal model.
3. Design specific actions necessary to change to the ideal model.
4. Continue to run the business while simultaneously changing it in the direction of the ideal model.

Changing the organization should take place in a series of steps. These steps begin with analyzing and subdividing the company into its components. A component is the smallest grouping of activities that are interrelated because they all are essential in producing a recognizable source of earnings or an identifiable cost or expense.

Another step is to compute the investment related to the activities tied up in plant and equipment, personnel, and so on. Once these steps have been taken, it becomes possible to evaluate whether the business activity identified by that component meets or can be changed to meet the specifications of the model. Test questions such as the following are answered with regard to each identified component. Is the currently realized return consistent with the strategic model? If not, are there controllable expenses or pricing factors that could be altered to bring it within specific return-on-investment standards? Is this area of business activity consistent with market areas identified within the strategic model as viable areas for future growth? These questions are typical of the many employed to decide whether each segregated activity should be expanded, shortened, changed, or eliminated in pursuing corporate development.

The implementation of Phase 5 contributes a quantum leap in productivity because of the depth of change involved.

Consolidation: Phase 6

Phase 6 is to stabilize and consolidate progress achieved during Phases 1 through 5 before recycling into another period of change.
The goals are to:

1. Critique the change effort to ensure that activities that have been implemented are being continued as planned.
2. Identify weaknesses that could not have been anticipated throughout the implementation and take corrective action to rectify them.
3. Monitor changes in the business environment (competition, price of raw materials, wage differentials, and so on) that may indicate that fundamental shifts in the model are necessary.

Three features of business suggest the importance of a consolidating phase in organization development. Managing change is the opposite of managing the tried and true. People tend to repeat the tried and true, but they may lose interest, convictions, or courage about something novel and unpredictable, and reduced effort may cause it to fail. A second reason to consolidate progress is that by continuing the study of what is new, additional improvement opportunities may add to organizational thrust. A third is that significant alterations in the outer environment may cause changes specified in the model and implemented in Phase 5 to be more or less favorable than had been anticipated.

Phase 6 strategies and instruments enable an organization to assess its current strengths and to build upon its gains. The monitoring activities of Phase 6 provide a basis for specifying needs for additional change. The significant aspect of Phase 6 is that the consolidation effort must be managed rather than left to its own momentum.

Many organizations—some very large—have reaped significant benefits once they installed the fundamental values of the Grid on a culture-wide basis.

SUMMARY

Principles of behavior come into use only when the values on which they rest are understood and appreciated. The Grid approach centers on teaching its theory and principles and then bringing leadership into line with them. Grid development presents a series of six phases of change as a fully integrated program.

From a behavioral point of view, Grid development brings individual effort into more effective teamwork and promotes the development of more effective interfaces between organization teams. From a business-system point of view, it enables organization members to design and implement a system of business logic and a corporate culture that are supportive of operational results and profit.

MAKING IT AT THE TOP: WHAT'S ABOVE THE BOTTOM LINE CONTROLS THE SIZE OF THE BOTTOM LINE

Previous chapters have presented the Grid framework of initiative, inquiry, advocacy, decision making, conflict solving, and critique, and concrete illustrations of how these concepts translate into operational practices at the top of organizations. Exercising leadership in each of the several styles has personal consequences for corporate heads and likely organizational consequences for corporate culture and philosophy and, eventually, the bottom line. It is in these ways that corporate culture, top leadership, and the bottom line are inextricably linked.

PROCESS ASPECTS OF CORPORATE LEADERSHIP

The preface drew attention to a distinction between content and process. The *content* side of leadership involves technical considerations such as financial analysis, manufacturing knowledge, and marketing know-how. The *process* side relates to the manner in which such knowledge and understanding is utilized in achieving concrete, bottom-line results with and through others. The various categories of technical knowledge are indispensable to good decision making and implementation, but they are relatively useless unless brought into effective operational decision making and implementation through sound processes of interaction between a leader and those in subordinate roles. This point of emphasis corrects an important bias present in corporate life for decades. The bias is that rational analysis of problems is the necessary and sufficient condition for solving them. Since we know that this is only a part of the story, the heretofore unacknowledged ingredient of process can contribute to problem solving and help reverse adverse productivity trends.

The general term *productivity* can be taken as an index that subsumes other indicators, i.e., profitability, return on investment, market penetration, or earnings per share. The conclusion is that reversing adverse productivity trends probably is possible only by factoring the unacknowledged ingredient of effective leadership processes into organization performance at all levels.

The production-people dichotomy is often dealt with in many unsatisfactory ways: 9,1, 1,9, 1,1, 5,5 styles, plus opportunism, facadism, and paternalism. However, there appears to be a best way for integrating people into production. Tables 13-1 and 13-2 give a summary of the options for exercising leadership in sound and unsound ways. The needed improvements in productivity trends can be expected when the 9,9 style of leadership is brought into more widespread use.

A BROADER PERSPECTIVE

When the 9,9 style characterizes the teamwork existing among the top leadership and has permeated the corporate culture and philosophy, bottom line consequences are likely to be positive. Many possible reasons for this are listed below. A 9,9 orientation is likely to:

1. Increase the use of human resources that are available in finding solutions to problems.
2. "Tune" more eyes and ears to seeing what really is going on in the

inner and outer environment of the company, therefore, fewer opportunities are likely to be missed.

3. Place fuller attention on digging out the underlying facts so that more understanding of the real issues comes to prevail.
4. Quicken the pace and enrich and expand the areas of organization life to which initiatives are applied. Thus as more problems are defined, the likelihood increases that more problems get solved.
5. Open up the number and quality of alternatives considered in searching for solutions to problems.
6. Produce better networking and processing of information to permit a deeper analysis of problems, clearer perception of their causes, and sharper proposals for their solutions.
7. Lift the energy level and quicken response time.

Some have thought what is involved here is joint decision making in which the boss shares power with subordinates. Such is not the case. While decisions may be deliberated to ensure full understanding of the problem to be solved and agreement on how it will be handled, the boss still may retain the decision-making authority. Many times, the character of responsibility assigned makes it impossible to do anything less. The issue is not joint decision making or power sharing. The issue is better, fuller, and deeper deliberation of the issues and problems that do have to be solved and that can benefit from open discussion. Determining which issues of management are best dealt with on a one-alone, one-to-one, or one-to-all basis can create a dilemma that, if not correctly resolved, can impede effectiveness. Though not directly germane to the issues dealt with here, the appendix provides a further discussion of these problems.

The 9,9 style can be a powerful force for moving a corporation forward. Some reasons follow:

1. By creating an image of the desired future, it becomes possible for members throughout the organization to see options and alternatives within the framework of the intended future.
2. Many external and internal business opportunities can be seized that otherwise might have been disregarded if an image of the future had been unavailable.
3. An organization has a greater likelihood of being able to anticipate and avoid hazards or, if adversity strikes, of being able to cope with it rapidly and creatively.
4. The character of corporate effort can be amended to meet unexpected but important changes in the marketing and other environments within which the corporation operates and by which it is influenced.

Table 13-1 Leadership Elements by Grid Style

Leadership Elements	Grid Style Descriptions					
	9,1	1,9	1,1	5,5	Paternalism	9,9
Initiative	I drive myself and others.	I initiate actions that help and support others.	I put out enough to get by.	I seek to maintain a steady pace.	I stress loyalty and extend appreciation to those who support my initiatives.	I exert vigorous effort and others join in enthusiastically.
Inquiry	I investigate facts, beliefs, and positions so that I am in control of any situation and to assure myself that others are not making mistakes.	I look for facts, beliefs, and positions that suggest all is well. For the sake of harmony, I am not inclined to challenge others.	I go along with facts, beliefs, and positions given to me.	I take things more or less at face value and check facts, beliefs, and positions when obvious discrepancies appear.	I double-check what others tell me and compliment them when I am able to verify their positions.	I search for and validate information. I invite and listen for opinions, attitudes, and ideas different than my own. I continuously reevaluate my own and others' facts, beliefs, and positions for soundness.
Advocacy	I stand up for my opinions, attitudes, and ideas even though it means rejecting others' views.	I embrace opinions, attitudes, and ideas of others even though I have reservations.	I keep my own counsel but respond when asked. I avoid taking sides by not revealing my opinions, attitudes, and ideas.	I express opinions, attitudes, and ideas in a tentative way and try to meet others halfway.	I maintain strong convictions but permit others to express their ideas so that I can help them think more objectively.	I feel it is important to express my concerns and convictions. I respond to ideas sounder than my own by changing my mind.

Conflict solving	When conflict arises I try to cut it off or win my position.	I avoid generating conflict, but when it appears I try to soothe feelings to keep people together.	I remain neutral or seek to stay out of conflict.	When conflict arises I try to find a reasonable position that others find suitable.	When conflict arises I terminate it but thank people for expressing their views.
					When conflict arises I seek out reasons for it in order to resolve underlying causes.
Decision making	I place high value on making my own decisions and am rarely influenced by others.	I search for decisions that maintain good relations and encourage others to make decisions when possible.	I let others make decisions or come to terms with whatever happens.	I search for workable decisions that others accept.	I have the final say and make a sincere effort to see that my decisions are accepted.
					I place high value on arriving at sound decisions. I seek understanding and agreement.
Critique	I pinpoint weaknesses or failure to measure up.	I give encouragement and offer praise when something positive happens but avoid giving negative feedback.	I avoid giving feedback.	I give informal or indirect feedback regarding suggestions for improvement.	I give others feedback and expect them to accept it because it is for their own good.
					I encourage two-way examination of how we do things and work together in order to strengthen operations by learning how to get better results.

Source: Robert R. Blake and Jane S. Mouton, Executive Grid Seminar Participant Materials. Austin, Texas: Scientific Methods, Inc., 1985. Reproduced by permission.

Table 13-2   Executive Grid Style and Corporate Culture

Culture Items	9.1	1.9	1.1	5.5	Paternalism	9.9
Authority	Authority is exercised through edicts, with minimum information provided concerning rationale; subordinates are expected to comply.	Praise and reassurance guide action. Reprimands are withheld if possible.	Requirements are passed down without follow-up.	Easygoing give-and-take permits authority to be exercised in an acceptable manner.	Those in higher positions know what is best for the organization and subordinates are expected to react in good spirits.	Authority is present, but use of it is nominal because people have a shared understanding of what needs to be done and are ready to apply sound effort in achieving it.
Objectives (planning)	Objectives come down with little opportunity for those who must implement to influence them.	Objectives are discussed but do not strongly affect people's actions; gaining or maintaining approval of others is more important.	Objectives are lacking and actions are based mostly on doing one thing at a time.	Objectives are based on forecasts, projections from past performance, or responses to unexpected changes.	People are expected to accept the objectives assigned them in a positive way.	People are involved in setting, reviewing, and evaluating those objectives on which their performance can have an impact.
Communication	Communication is one-way on a need-to-know basis; little feedback is sought from subordinates or others.	Social and nonwork topics are typical of pleasant, on-the-job conversation; discussion of work content is secondary.	People get the word on a "message passing" basis; little or no in-depth discussion of on-the-job activities occurs.	People filter what they say consistent with organization expectations. Negative feelings appear as innuendo and gossip.	People are told what to do in ways that encourage their acquiescence.	People are well-informed and participate in problem analysis and decision making; needed information is communicated up, down, and sideways on a two-way basis.
Conflict	Rank is used to cut off conflict and to decide between different viewpoints.	Conflict is relieved by yielding, placating, and looking for the positive side.	People avoid taking positions that would provoke conflict or becoming involved in those which exist.	People sense when they have pushed their positions far enough and back off as necessary to meet others halfway.	Conflict is focused upon strongly, since it is expected that people are not only obedient but loyal.	Points of disagreement are made explicit and reasons for them are identified to resolve underlying causes.

Coordination (between components)	Coordination is mostly through the formal chain of command.	Frequent visiting and friendliness between persons result in each knowing what help can be requested from another with certainty of acceptance.	Cooperation between organization components is minimal.	Cooperation is based more on tradition, precedent, and personality than on the nature of the tasks to be performed.	Coordination is from above but efforts are made to see that working arrangements are acceptable to those affected.	Cooperation is based on the nature of tasks and ways that maximize effective interaction.
Critique	Critique by inspection permits performance to be pinpointed for weaknesses or failure to measure up; acceptable performance is expected and rarely discussed when it occurs.	People are urged to do their best and are complimented for effort, but failures are rarely discussed.	There is little or no use made of critique.	Informal checks are made; postmortems let people deal with their tensions but have only minor effect on future activities.	Praise is offered when something positive happens; reprimands are to stop negative actions.	Critiques of performance are for reviewing how activities are being managed in order to strengthen them in the future.
Commitment	Apart from commitment related to personal belief in organization objectives, people resent their inability to leave.	Positive feelings toward the organization arise from the enjoyment employment makes possible.	Staying in the organization comes from the conclusion that it is more convenient or less painful to remain than leave.	Commitment arises from the prestige of being a member of a "good organization."	People learn that when they discharge their obligations and duties as expected, they will be taken care of.	Gratification comes from making needed contributions to the organization on a spontaneous and voluntary basis.
Productivity	Pressure for more output is more or less constant.	Even those who are not fully and productively occupied are retained (or reassigned) to avoid upsetting morale.	Doing the minimum on the job is common.	Acceptable levels of productivity are maintained which can be attained without placing people under undue pressure.	Productivity is expected and people who submit to demands placed upon them are rewarded.	People are personally committed on an individual basis and as team members to being fully productive.

(Continued)

Table 13–2 *(Continued)*

Culture Items	9,1	1,9	1,1	5,5	Paternalism	9,9
Cost consciousness	People are pressured to minimize costs in their decisions and actions.	Maintaining a warm and congenial environment prevails over cost consciousness.	There is little evidence of cost consciousness.	Efforts at cost containment are present but reduced by consideration of convenience.	Cost consciousness is emphasized and people are shown appreciation for compliance.	Cost consciousness is a way of life, but not an end in itself. Costs relative to benefits guide people's thinking about the activities for which they are responsible.
Creativity	Suggestions or novel ideas are only resisted; through dogged determination is resistance overcome.	Ideas are listened to appreciatively though implementation is unlikely.	New ideas or approaches are rarely pursued.	New ideas are most acceptable when they represent views of the majority and extensions and modifications of current policies, procedures, or practices.	Even though held out as a positive value, new ways of doing things are not welcomed.	Creativity and innovation are stimulated by openness and the readiness to experiment.

Source: Robert R. Blake and Jane S. Mouton, Executive Grid Seminar Participant Materials. Austin, Texas: Scientific Methods, Inc., 1985. Reproduced by permission.

These constitute the process issues that are present in a corporate culture of excellence. As can be seen, they have little or nothing to do with the content problems that have to be solved. Their impact upon content problems is indirect, through better involvement, deeper commitment, better teamwork, more thorough inquiry, more open and candid advocacy, and more confrontational conflict solving. Possibly the most important impact of all comes from learning by experience through diligent use of critique.

Salary and benefits can help unlock human resources, but they won't necessarily bring human resources to bear on developing a more profitable corporation. Architecture and decor can make a building a more attractive place in which to work but not necessarily a more productive one. The same goes for better tools and equipment, flexible working hours, and so on.

All these can help. But the real key to using them in the most productive way is to get organization members involved in and committed to corporate success. Executive leadership that fosters this kind of involvement and commitment on a widespread basis is the kind that makes it at the top through achievements reflected in the bottom line.

APPENDIX

TACTICS OF 9,9 TEAMWORK

Leading effective teamwork is a significant aspect of the manager's behavior because the 9,9 orientation embraces the concern for integrating the needs and views of people into production.

GUIDELINES FOR INCLUSION

The 9,9 orientation approaches problem solving and decision making by encouraging thorough inquiry and strong advocacy from everyone who is involved. The phrase "everyone who is involved" pinpoints the need to examine the issue of inclusion more closely.

Guidelines that clarify when to use 1/0, 1/1, or 1/all decision making are introduced in the accompanying table. These guidelines answer the question, "Under what conditions are 1/0, 1/1, 1/some, or 1/all approaches

171

Testing Actions for When They Should Be 1/0, 1/1, or 1/all

Criteria	Approach		
	1/0 If	1/1 If	1/All (or 1/Some) If
1. Responsibility for the problem	My problem	His or her problem; our problem	Our problem
2. Time to contact	Unavailable	Available	Available
3. Judgmental competence	Full	Low	Insufficient
4. Pooling of information	Unnecessary	Vertical or horizontal	Needed both horizontally and vertically
5. Synergy	Not possible	Possible	Possible
6. Critique	No one else	Problem belonging to two people	Problem with implications for all
7. Significance to the team	Low	Low	High
8. Involvement and commitment of others	No significance	Helpful or essential	Necessary or essential
9. Relevance for others	None	Present	Present
10. Understanding by others of purpose or rationale of decision	No need or can be assumed	Needed	Needed
11. Coordination of effort	Unnecessary	Vertical or horizontal	Horizontal and vertical
12. Change in team norms and standards	Not relevant	Not relevant	Relevant
13. Representation of issue in other settings	None	Pertinent	Pertinent
14. Delegation	Possible	Unlikely	Unlikely
15. Management development	None	Present	Present

Source: Grid Team Building, Scientific Methods, Inc., Austin, Texas, 1984. Reproduced by permission.

likely to be most effective?" The left-hand column identifies criteria that help a manager decide if 1/0, 1/1, or 1/all is the soundest basis of action. The conditions for 1/some are so similar to 1/all that they are not separated for discussion, but these are actions that involve more than 1/1 but less than 1/all, where "all" means the entire membership of the team.

A boss should act without consulting others when the criteria for good decision making and problem solving, shown on the left, match the conditions in the 1/0 column. When conditions match entries in the second column, 1/1 actions should occur. When the circumstances match those in the column to the right, 1/some or 1/all actions should be taken.

The first six criteria relate most closely in one way or another to maximizing the quality of decision making by the effective and efficient use of human resources.

1. Responsibility for the Problem

If, in viewing a problem, an individual can say, "That problem is my sole responsibility, and I have the capacity to handle it," then the problem calls for 1/0 action and the exercise of self-reliant initiative. If, however, the individual lacks the capacity for handling the problem or if it overlaps the responsibilities of two people, it represents a 1/1 situation. If the problem is superordinate in the sense that each individual has a piece of the problem but no one has all of it, then 1/all is the best interaction for solving it.

2. Time to Contact

If there is no time to involve others, for whatever sound reason, the individual takes the necessary action on a solo, or 1/0, basis. If consulting others will be advantageous and time is available to consult with one but not all, then it is a 1/1 situation. If time is available and there are advantages to several being involved, then it is 1/some or 1/all.

3. Judgmental Competence

A manager may have the depth and experience to exercise sound judgment. Other things being equal, this is done in a 1/0 way. If the manager's experience in the field of a certain problem is insufficient, however, and one other person is needed to strengthen the soundness of judgment, the situation is 1/1. If reaching a sound judgment requires the participation of everyone, then it should be carried out in a 1/all team manner.

4. Pooling of Information

When all of the information needed to execute an action is possessed by one individual, 1/0 action is appropriate. If two people each have some of the information needed for the total understanding of a situation, then pooling of information may be required on a 1/1 basis. This may be a boss-subordinate relationship or it may be between equal-level colleagues. When all team members have unique aspects of information that need to be pooled to develop total comprehension, then 1/all pooling may be required.

5. Synergy

The term *synergy* applies when thrashing through of all the perspectives of team members results in a better solution than any one, two, or several members might have developed. Teamwork may be needed because of the synergistic possibilities from several or all team members' studying or reviewing a problem. The leader who hears the opinions of subordinates in the presence of others gains the maximum opportunity for access to their thinking. Disagreements, rationale for positions, reservations, and so on are stimulated under this kind of open leadership. However, 1/0 is the rule if no synergy can be anticipated, and 1/1 if only one other member can contribute.

6. Critique

Decision quality may be strengthened by discussions that study team skills in solving problems. If a problem has no team-building application, it should be studied in a 1/0 way by self-critique, in a 1/1 manner if two people can learn something about teamwork effectiveness from it, and in a 1/all way if the full team can benefit from studying it. In addition, there are many techniques of critique that aid team members to study results relative to performance. These are detailed elsewhere both in this book and in others.

The next critical criteria, Numbers 7 through 13, are more closely related to the acceptance issue, that is, the readiness of team members to implement a decision once it has been made.

7. Significance to the Team

If the action has no team implications beyond one member alone, it should be handled 1/0 unless he or she does not carry it out. If it has far-reaching operational significance, such as shifting the reporting lines in the organization, then the entire team should understand the issues. The greater the significance of an action for changing team purpose, direction, character, or procedures, the more desirable the participation and involvement of all members.

8. Involvement and Commitment of Others

Understanding the problem and its solution may be necessary to achieve acceptance from those who must implement the decision. If the action to be taken does not involve other team members, it should be made 1/0. If it affects only one other, discussion with this team member is necessary (1/1). When the action has team-wide implications, all should discuss the pros and cons until those whose interests are involved have full understanding. Doubts and reservations are then relieved, and everyone is in a position of agreement and support.

9. Relevance for Others

Those whose future actions will be affected by a decision need to think through the issue and discuss its implications to see that they understand and are committed to it. The larger the number of team members who have personal stakes in an action, the greater the need for them to discuss the decision.

10. Understanding by Others of Purpose or Rationale of Decision

There are some kinds of problems to which others cannot contribute, yet they can benefit from an awareness of the rationale employed in analyzing or solving it. When others already know the rationale or when it is not important to them, then the action should be 1/0. However, sometimes the rationale behind the action will benefit at least one other; therefore, it may need to be dealt with in a 1/1 way. All the others may not be in a position to contribute to a solution but may need to know the rationale, and under these circumstances the rationale should be communicated on a 1/all basis.

11. Coordination of Effort

Often an action can and should be 1/0 because there is no need for coordination. When coordination is required, the matter should be dealt with jointly, on a 1/1 basis. Sometimes several if not all team members are involved in implementing a decision; in that case the strategies for coordination need to be worked out on a 1/all basis.

12. Change in Team Norms and Standards

Norms and standards that influence performance on a within-team basis may need to be established, modified, or completely changed. All team members need to be involved for them to know and be committed to the new norms and standards. Because each team member adheres to team-based norms and standards, it is unlikely that a 1/0 action would shift a norm. The most favorable condition for reaching such decisions is where a new team norm is explicitly agreed to by all team members, particularly if the new norm is intended to replace or modify an existing one.

13. Representation of an Issue in Other Settings

Sometimes one team member serves as a representative in settings outside his or her own team situation. Other team members may contribute little or nothing to a decision, but because they need to know what is under consideration, they are brought in to increase their own understanding.

The next two items are concerned specifically with using teamwork situations for management development.

14. Delegation

A problem should be solved by a person of lesser rank if he or she has the understanding and judgment necessary to deal with it, or if to do so would strengthen the subordinate's managerial effectiveness. Thus, capacity for exercising responsibility by dealing with larger and larger problems is increased. This shifts a 1/0 from one member to another. In addition, the boss is free to utilize this time on matters only he or she can solve.

The principle here is: other things being equal, delegation should be relied on when (1) subordinates can deal with a given problem as well as or better than the boss; (2) the subordinate can strengthen managerial effectiveness; (3) delegation, not abdication, is the motivation that propels the boss in this direction; (4) the time made available to the boss permits the solution of another problem more important than the delegated one; and (5) the conditions are such that the subordinate has reasonable prospects of success.

15. Management Development

Team members participate in analyzing managerial issues, even though they may have little to contribute to the quality of management by way of information and even though their acceptance of a decision about an issue is immaterial. Their participation is to enable them to gain knowledge and to develop the judgment needed for dealing with such problems in the future. If a problem has no management development implications, it should be dealt with 1/0; if it has management development implications for only one other, it should be dealt with 1/1; if it has management development implications for all team members, it should be dealt with 1/all.

Matrix Teamwork

The matrix concept of organization has been of increasing interest in recent years. With matrix teamwork at least two differently structured arrangements are possible. In one a subordinate may have more than one boss, such as a line reporting relationship and a functional specialty reporting arrangement. In another, any member may belong, often on a temporary basis but sometimes more or less permanently, to more than one team, such as a project team, a marketing launch team, or some other kind of interdepartmental grouping.

Matrix-centered structures place even greater emphasis on teamwork, as a member may join in to contribute specialized expertise, then leave. If unable to work effectively with others, a member's contribution is likely to be reduced or completely cancelled. Additionally, the member who cannot resolve tensions that arise from having two bosses also may be compelled to work at a level of reduced effectiveness.

Matrix teamwork involving 9,9 participation skills enables members to contribute to organization effectiveness in a significant way. The fifteen criteria for answering the question, "Who should participate?" are equally pertinent to composing a matrix-centered team.

INDEX

ABOUT THE AUTHORS

ROBERT BLAKE is the author of over thirty books, including *The Managerial Grid*, which has sold over one million copies and is available in ten languages. Dr. Blake is a pioneer in organizational dynamics and initiated the first organizational development program in a major American corporation. A former Fulbright scholar, Dr. Blake has lectured at Harvard, Oxford, and Cambridge universities, and has served as a consultant in forty countries. He is chairman of Scientific Methods, Inc.

JANE MOUTON holds degrees in mathematics and psychology. In addition to work in executive management and organization development, she has engaged in research on the dynamics of win-lose conflict and creative decision making. She is the coauthor with Robert Blake of over thirty books, including *Synergogy, Solving Costly Organizational Conflicts*, and *The Managerial Grid III*. Dr. Mouton is president of Scientific Methods, Inc.